PROTESTANT PIONEERS
IN KOREA

The American Society of Missiology Series, in collaboration with Orbis Books, seeks to publish scholarly works of high merit and wide interest on numerous aspects of missiology—the study of mission. Able presentations on new and creative approaches to the practice and understanding of mission will receive close attention.

American Society of Missiology Series, No. 1

PROTESTANT PIONEERS IN KOREA

Everett Nichols Hunt, Jr.

ORBIS BOOKS
Maryknoll, New York 10545

The Catholic Foreign Mission Society of America (Maryknoll) recruits and trains people for overseas missionary service. Through Orbis Books Maryknoll aims to foster the international dialogue that is essential to mission. The books published, however, reflect the opinions of their authors and are not meant to represent the official position of the society.

Library of Congress Cataloging in Publication Data

Hunt, Everett Nichols.
  Protestant pioneers in Korea.

  Bibliography: p.
  1. Missions—Korea—History. 2. Protestant
churches—Missions—History. I. Title.
BV3460.H86   266'.0095 19   79-27089
ISBN 0-88344-396-1

Published by Orbis Books, Maryknoll, NY 10545, in collaboration with the American Society of Missiology

Contents

Preface to the Series

The purpose of the ASM Series is to publish, without regard for disciplinary, national, or denominational boundaries, scholarly works of high quality and wide interest on missiological themes from the entire spectrum of scholarly pursuits, e.g., theology, history, anthropology, sociology, linguistics, health, education, art, political science, economics, and development, to articulate but a partial list. Always the focus will be on Christian mission.

By "mission" in this context is meant a cross-cultural passage over the boundary between faith in Jesus Christ and its absence. In this understanding of mission, the basic functions of Christian proclamation, dialogue, witness, service, fellowship, worship, and nurture are of special concern. How does the transition from one cultural context to another influence the shape and interaction of these dynamic functions?

Missiologists know that they need the other disciplines. And other disciplines, we dare to suggest, need missiology, perhaps more than they sometimes realize. Neither the insider's nor the outsider's view is complete in itself. The world Christian mission has through two millennia amassed a rich and well-documented body of experience to share with other disciplines.

Interaction will be the hallmark of this Series. It desires to be a channel for talking to one another instead of about one another. Secular scholars and church-related missiologists have too long engaged in a sterile venting of feelings about one another, often lacking in full evidence. Ignorance of and indifference to one another's work has been no less harmful to good scholarship.

We express our warm thanks to various mission agencies whose financial contributions enabled leaders of vision in the ASM to launch this new venture. The future of the ASM series will, we feel sure, fully justify their confidence and support.

William J. Danker, Chairperson,
ASM Series Editorial Committee

Foreword

Right off, on page one, Everett Hunt sets the proper context for his writing, so far as historians are concerned. He quotes a former president of the American Historical Association, who staked out mission history as a "great and underused research laboratory" in the field of international and intercultural relations. Then Hunt sets out to work in that laboratory and present some findings.

To people who stand in the tradition of missionary life, such an assertion about an "underused laboratory" must sound incredible. For almost two centuries in the Protestant world—and before that, in Catholic Reformation days of Francis Xavier the same circumstances prevailed—we have had stories, histories, diaries, journals, novels, sermons, and goals all growing out of the experience of Christian missions. How can the field be "underused" and underdeveloped?

In a way, of course, it has not been. Those who inspire and promote missions, as well as those who profit from their outreach, have no problems about the invisibility of the enterprise. But they often forget that they belong to a subculture, a zone of life as carefully bounded as a fraternal organization or a cabal. The larger society, the one we like to call secular and pluralist, lives with little information and some misinformation about the whole enterprise. To them the true accounting of missionary history is unknown or, at best, arcane, as if in a foreign language about "old, unhappy, far-off things, and battles long ago."

The larger society misses much by not knowing the story of missions, and particularly books like this one that speak of Christian intrusions on fresh territory. That society goes about its business of trading with other nations, warring or making peace, blundering and serving in them, being their victim and wanting to be their friend, oblivious to the story of how so many relations between nations got started and what sustained them. They are puzzled by the talented anti-Western leaders who were shaped in missionary schools, or are unaware of the contributions to health (and thus to problems of overpopulation and the like) made by missionary clinics and hospitals.

I have spoken of misinformation; it is often based on prejudices that have been well tended and well fed in our Western societies. Thanks to James Michener's book *Hawaii*, I like to speak of this as Michenerism. This stereotype shows the world as a set of serene anthropological zoos that would have endured until the End had not snooping and sniping Christian missionaries invaded. Other cultures were seen to be thought-out zones of religious commitment, which meddlesome and pushy missionaries could not wait to blast apart. The missionary was nothing but a chaplain to the capitalist exploiter, nothing but the handholder to the imperialist, nothing but the prompter of Western colonialism.

Enough "nothing buttery." Missionaries have at times been saints but they have just as often been as venal and corrupt or, worse, as shortsighted as the general run of Christians, be they pastors or lay. Their faults are patent. But their virtues have had less chance to show. More important, their actual situation has been obscured and dimmed by the Micheners and their kith. The quaint old cultures would have been disrupted five or ten minutes later than the arrival of missionaries in any case. And the disruptions would have come from mere exploiters, capitalist or technological or socialist—it makes no difference. But the Christians at least frequently came quietly, gently, offering an alternative order and hope in the face of cultural shock.

Everett Hunt belongs to that new generation of historians who blend their missionary genetic strains with their scholarly development in the secular and pluralist academic world. This new breed is neither so defensive about missionary mama and papa that they must reject the university, nor so aggressive against them that they must be oedipal and jettison their Christian lineage. Hunt moves with ease between these worlds, making a ceaseless effort to understand.

The laboratory he works in, Korea, is of particular importance for these new inquiries. A century ago it was closed to the West and Christian witness. A half century ago it was well on its way to being the most "Christianized" nation in Asia. As one reads these pages on readiness for mission, it seems as if a venture a half century earlier would have met with nothing but Great Wall resistance and exclusion. A half century later would have been too late. Korea would have made up its mind and modernized without allowing for the Christian witness. Must one believe that the Holy Spirit set the right time, a kairos, and sent the strange and often frail heroes of Hunt's story as his agents? Fortunately, the historian need not decide something on such a theological scale.

Hunt sets out to do, and partly fails to do, what all historians try and in tasks at which they all in part fail. He attempts to understand and explain how and why something worked when and where it did, though all odds were against it. In the end human motivation, at least on a culturewide scale, is too complex to allow for fully satisfying sortings-out and accountings. But one can move past mere educated guesses, as this book does. Hunt knows all the theses, primitive and sophisticated, about methods and cultural readiness, and takes them seriously. But he knows that history could have been different, no matter what the theory, had the wrong doctor made the wrong move in respect to the wrong member of the royal family. He knows that savvy missionaries lunged at every kind of opportunity to do what the situation demanded by way of healing or teaching, so long as they could serve—and get started. But he knows that the total of these reckonings do not give us the Big Explanation.

Just as I began by mentioning Hunt's first lines, I conclude by mentioning his last ones. In a comment on the sources, he mentions his frustration over the paucity of revelations or even observations at all in the Korean sources. I picture him on the scene still probing, digging, hoping that one day he will turn up materials that will help tell the side of the missionized people. Until then we shall content ourselves with this probing effort to go as far as Western sources permit. This is in part familiar territory, revisited. But it will be a new trip for most readers. And there are enough new discoveries to beckon the veteran voyagers on the scene of misionary history; they will find new horizons for their own future exploration.

Martin E. Marty

Acknowledgments

I am grateful to Oriental Missionary Society International for giving me wholehearted support during the period of my studies. Dr. John Chongnahm Cho, president of Seoul Theological Seminary, also gave his enthusiastic permission.

My professors at the University of Chicago Divinity School had a profound influence on my thinking and the course of my study. I want to thank Professor R. Pierce Beaver, under whose guidance I began my program; Professor Joseph M. Kitagawa, dean of Divinity School; and Professor Akira Iriye in the history department of the university. Special thanks are due to Professor Martin E. Marty, my thesis adviser, who gave generously of his time and friendship.

I would also like to thank my parents, Reverend and Mrs. Everett N. Hunt, who helped me in so many ways. Their pride in my work often exceeded my accomplishments and spurred me to renewed effort.

My daughter, Julie, put up with an absent father for much of three years yet always made me feel she understood. And my wife, Carroll, was my editor, typist, sounding board, and strongest supporter. I stole much of her own writing time to make all this possible. Yet she always gave me more.

To all, my deep appreciation and love.

Introduction

Academic historians are showing increased interest in the missionary and the whole mission enterprise as an important facet of international and intercultural relations. In such studies the missionary is viewed as a person in two worlds. John King Fairbank observed, "Mission history is a great and underused research laboratory for the comparative observation of cultural stimulus and response in both directions" (1969:878).

Ernest R. May and James C. Thomson, in their introductory volume to a series from Harvard on American–East Asian relations, go so far as to say, "Missionaries formed the principal channel for a two-way process of cultural influence between East and West" (1972:16). Still another student of American–East Asian relations, Kwang Ching Liu, notes, "Nothing in modern history is in greater need of analysis than the missionary movement, in both its causes and effects" (1963:13).

Until recently studies of the missionaries were largely concerned with their role in the propagation of the gospel. These studies paralleled closely the same path as the missionaries. That is to say, the studies followed them as they left the home country behind, arrived in the new country (the mission field), and began to preach. Of course, "preach" came to mean different things in different countries and in different stages of the mission, but missionaries were agents of the church's worldwide mission and were studied mainly by those sympathetic to their cause.

The missionaries, particularly the pioneer missionaries in any country, often played a wider role than just "preaching the gospel." If it be true that first impressions are often lasting ones, the initial encounter between the missionaries and their new country of vocation was significant.

There are many studies of this initial encounter, as well as important stages along the way for China and Japan in the East Asian world (Fairbank 1974). Similar studies for Korea are few.

General bibliographies in American–East Asian studies indicate a much larger proportion of preoccupation with China and somewhat less for Japan. Studies of Korean–American relations are extremely limited. The reasons for this need not be a concern here. The fact simply represents one of the underlying reasons for this study.

This is not an attempt to study the whole of Protestant mission history in Korea. Rather, the focus is on the period of beginnings: specifically, from the arrival of Horace Newton Allen in September 1884, until 1890, when mission work was well established.

1

Compared to Korea's East Asian neighbors, China and Japan, both the beginnings and the later Protestant presence in Korea may be considered more impressive. Indeed, Korea has been referred to as the success story in modern missions.

Explanations for the "success" of Protestant beginnings in Korea have become cliché. Most commonly they are: (1) the purity of the gospel preached by the missionaries; (2) the use of the Nevius method (see below, p. 77); (3) the response of the Koreans. What one fails to hear is the recognition that the same "pure gospel" when preached in China and Japan failed to evoke the response that has been so abundantly evident in Korea. In regard to the Nevius method, it was used only by the Presbyterians and was not adopted as official mission policy until 1891, fully seven years after the arrival of the first resident Protestant missionary. By this time the period of beginnings was over and the Protestant presence was well established. Furthermore, the Nevius Plan in and of itself is not sufficient explanation for growth or nongrowth even in areas where supposedly it was official mission policy (Shearer 1966). As for the third explanation, "the response of the Koreans," this is more a statement of fact than an explanation.

Missionaries have been recognized as "the most pervasive expression of America's nineteenth century sense of mission, contributing to mutually favorable relations between the country in which they served and America" (Beaver 1967). Friendly relations between Korea and America were evident from their beginning in 1882. Protestant missionaries arrived in Korea so soon after the "opening" that they played a more significant role in shaping Korea's image of America than their counterparts in China or Japan. Missionaries in China and Japan were kept carefully secluded in treaty ports and commercial centers far from the seat of government authority. In Seoul, the first Protestant missionary, a doctor, lived in housing very near the palace of the king and was given as his first patient the king's own nephew. Since all of this was happening just over two years after the arrival of America's Envoy Extraordinary and Minister Plenipotentiary to the Korean court, it served to strengthen Korea's already favorable impression of America's disinterested benevolence.

At the same time, in helping to shape America's image of Korea, the missionaries played an important part. In China, men on clipper ships brought back images long before there was a significant reporting American Protestant missionary presence there. In Japan as well, merchants and diplomats were the first image-makers. In Korea, though the diplomats preceded them by two years, almost immediately on their arrival the missionaries began writing with a conscious desire to inform the supporting constituency back home of the nature of this new area they were taking for God.

It may be assumed that missionaries were more culturally sensitive and thus would be good reporters. Not only were they educated, they went to these countries with a special alertness to cultural traits and racial characteristics. It was in this very area of culture contact that the missionaries were to do their work. Uniquely in Korea, because they were welcomed into the heart of the capital city and permitted to live in close proximity to the seat of power of the Korean court, they were in the best possible vantage point for reporting.

This reporting was a conscious attempt on the part of the missionaries both to create an image of Korea for Americans and to strengthen the American sense of mission. Fairbank suggested that for the early days of mission activity in China the impact of the missionary was greater on the United States than it was on China (May and Thomson 1972:28). Impact is difficult to measure. However, the missionaries in Korea, because they arrived so early in Korean–American relations, were in a position to make an impact at home and in their new country of vocation.

Protestant beginnings in Korea occurred at a time of remarkable convergence of various factors. This convergence provided a context in which the missionaries were able to establish themselves, advance the cause of the gospel, and at the same time shape the Korean image of America and Americans. Simultaneously, by their aggressive reporting the missionaries helped to shape the American image of Korea and, because of their early "success," strengthen America's confidence in its God-ordained mission to evangelize the world.

Our first concern will be to look at the nature of Protestant beginnings in Korea. Who were the pioneers? How were they shaped? What was the nature of their early work? They were part of the late nineteenth-century missionary expansion from America. We will seek to show that the permission for missionaries to reside in a kingdom proscribing propagation of Christianity acknowledged their discretion in engaging only in those activities which would make tangible contribution to the needs of the Korean people. At the same time their quiet building of relationships of confidence later made the proscription a dead letter and their presence officially recognized and honored by the court and the populace.

The court recognized that Protestant Christianity was an integral part of American life and thus desirable for Korea as it sought to build a stronger relationship with America. The king also was anxious to provide significant help for his people suffering from repeated epidemics of unknown and unchecked physical ills. Initially Christianity was accepted more for what Korean officialdom perceived it to be—nationally, internationally, and pragmatically—than anything inherent in Christianity or the specific approach of the missionaries. On an official level this was true, while unofficially people were being treated for their ills, provided with new educational opportunity, and some were being converted. Prolonged contact with the missionaries and deeper acquaintance with their gospel brought into being a growing Christian community finding felt needs met and life given new meaning and hope.

Concurrent with attempting to Christianize Korea, the missionaries were concerned to inform and inspire the constituency in America. Particularly those supporting the enterprise were anxious to see "results." If the missionary could report numbers of converts won, churches, schools, and hospitals established, tracts distributed and Scriptures translated and made available to the people, it greatly encouraged the folks back home. This reporting, however, was more than just a pragmatic concern for more funds and personnel. The missionaries were aware of the responsibility they shared for building the image of Korea in the minds of Americans. Further, it was an attempt to show how God was bringing success in this new advance of his kingdom on earth, and thereby encourage even more support in the work of building the church. Both missionary and supporter back home were convinced this was Christ's final great command to the church and the necessary condition for his expected return. Thus the task of world evangelization was one of utmost urgency.

The responsibility for this reportive function was urged on them both by board secretaries in New York and by their own awareness that they were now citizens of two worlds—dedicated to both for the cause of Christ but not fully a member of either. To Korea they were propagators; to America they were propagandizers. In both it was a religious motivation which urged them to fill the role. It was a conscious self-image which made them responsible for preaching and promoting.

Underlying the whole endeavor was a theological perspective without which the determining dynamic of this missionary activity may not be fully understood. The missionary was aware of cultural, social, psychological, and political forces working both for and against that mission. What gave the ultimate meaning to the whole enterprise was the theological framework in which the missionary viewed it. Those who chose not to go as missionaries themselves but instead sent a substitute, were motivated ultimately by the same theological concerns. This lifted the whole encounter between Christianity and Korea out of a mere space/time framework and gave a sense of eternal ultimacy to the task.

1

Korea, America, and Protestants:
First Contacts

Korea in East Asia

The Christian message is never introduced in a vacuum. The introduction of Protestant Christianity to Korea can only be fully understood in relation to certain key factors in the Asian–Korean context.

Korea for centuries held a firm place in the East Asian world. Situated geographically between China and Japan, it reflected the Confucian-based cultural influence of China.

This East Asian world was based on the Confucian model of the family. Thus Korea looked with respect to China as the "older brother" rather than an equal partner in a legally binding treaty. Until late in the nineteenth century a multiplicity of tributary relationships between China and Korea strengthened these Confucian family ties (Fairbank 1968:90-112).

From the beginning of the Yi Dynasty in Korea (1392) Confucianism not only served as the basis of relationships with China but also provided the ideological base for Korea's rulers as well. Though Confucianism strengthened Korea's place in the East Asian world during the early years of the Yi Dynasty, internal factionalism later grew to be a problem. It is a moot point how much Confucianism contributed to this. In the main, factions were not formed over differing interpretations of Confucian teachings but on problems of succession, pro- and anti-government feelings, regionalism, and family loyalties. Each faction would reinterpret Confucian teaching to form its own ideological base (Henderson and Yang 1958:81-101; 1959:259-76; Nelson 1946).

For the subsequent introduction of Christianity to Korea, one party that emerged in this period of factionalism was more important than any other, the Silhakpa, or Practical Learning School. The Silhaks were the most independent and original group of scholars in early modern Korean history. They criticized neo-Confucianism by applying a systematic kind of textual criticism to a study of the writings. They applied the inductive method to the study of history, phonetics, and etymology.

The Silhaks represented a "rebellion against primarily deductive, literary, and abstruse methods of thought." As a result they were "somewhat closer to western and scientific viewpoints than were the neo-Confucian schools" and "more open to western influence and methodology" (Henderson and Yang 1959:268).

The Practical Learning School was potentially disturbing to the Confucian-based traditional status quo. It no longer felt bound by rigid, traditional Confucian interpretations for the support of each new government policy. It encouraged a freer spirit of inquiry and a positive role for dissenting groups. At the same time, however, disunity and strife among people unable to cope with ideological differences of opinion became a problem. What might have provided a more favorable climate for initial contacts with the West instead fanned domestic strife and confusion, and a paralyzing inability to cope with new movements in international relations.

Initial Encounter: Korea and America

America's involvement in Asia began in the late eighteenth century with merchants and trade (Dennett 1963, 1922). Merchants were followed by diplomats whose primary function was the protection of America's trading rights. Finally the missionaries seeking new areas yet unreached with the gospel found their way first to China, then Japan.

Though centrally located in the East Asian world, Korea was somewhat removed from the shipping lanes used by merchant ships en route to China and Japan. Thus the country's awareness of the ever increasing American presence in Asia was secondhand.

Much of America's involvement in East Asia in the nineteenth century must be seen in relation to European nations, France and England in particular. While not interested in establishing colonial empires in Asia, America was interested in securing equal access to the potentially large market believed to be found in Asia. Thus successes and failures of other Western nations in Asia increased America's awareness and its desire to play a role, however dimly perceived that role may have been.

Meanwhile, China and Japan were sensitive not only to their own relations to Western powers but to the early Western contacts with Korea. Traditionally both a cultural bridge and a geographical buffer zone, Korea's international relations would affect for good or ill the balance of relationships in East Asia. Thus both from national self-interest as well as response to Korea's appeals for help, China and Japan each maneuvered to play a determinative role in Korea's emergence from seclusion.

The most strategic factor in Korea's internationalization was the signing of the treaty of Kangwha with Japan in 1876 (Conroy 1960). Japan's entry into relations with Western nations had started more than twenty years before. Following the beginnings in 1854, the treaty with America, there was progressive westernization in Japan. Significantly, when Japan sought to establish regular treaty relations with Korea, it was the treaty between Japan and the United States it used for a model.

As Japan was making aggressive moves in Asia and implementing Western ideas faster than any other Asian nation, China was seeking to maintain the traditional status quo. This was particularly true with relations between China and Korea. China not only insisted upon Korea's continued acceptance of a vassal relationship but also wanted Korea to make this known to any nations seeking relations with it. China's foreign policymaker, Li Hung Chang, was committed to maintaining peace in Asia. "Preservation of peace in Asia was preservation of the status quo in the relation between China and Korea" (Lin 1935–36).

When America began official diplomatic maneuvers to establish treaty relations with Korea, Li saw a chance to strengthen China's position. With both Japan and Russia taking a more aggressive interest in Korea it was in his best interest to keep Korea peaceful and neutral, a buffer between China and other nations.

If Korea would seek to strengthen itself, it could stand as a match for the Western intruders. At the same time, Li felt that a treaty between Korea and the United States would strengthen China by keeping other Western powers in balance in Korea. "In Li's estimate the United States had no territorial design and was the most reliable of the western nations" (Kim and Kim 1967:19).

Meanwhile the Korean king showed a growing awareness that foreign relations were changing and it was time for a restudy in the light of the new situation. "For our country to unite with the U.S. . . . . is a good plan. To this end if they continue to seek relations we will respond. If their ships come here for such a purpose we will receive them" (KS II:183-86; SJWIG 1880).

Treaty Relations Established

It was Admiral Shufeldt who urged the United States government to establish relations with Korea. After months of difficult negotiations he signed the treaty of Chemulpo. The ceremonies included planting the American flag and playing a verse of "Yankee Doodle." The date was May 22, 1881 (Shufeldt January 28, 1887 in Appenzeller Corr.; TMKG 1882; ISN 1882; MGTSSG 1882; CCIG 1882; Paullin 1910:470-99). The treaty was transmitted by President Arthur to the Senate on July 29, 1882, and ratified on January 9, 1883. Ratifications were exchanged in Seoul, May 19, and the treaty proclaimed on June 4, 1883 (SJWIG; ISN; KS 1883). American Minister Foote was already at the Korean capital. He had been received by the king and queen with distinction and courtesy.

When Foote's ship arrived in the harbor at Chemulpo, an official party boarded to extend welcome in behalf of the king. Responding to the significance of the occasion, the ship's crew ran up a Korean flag they had made and gave it a twenty-one-gun salute. After the salute its meaning was explained to the Koreans. "All agreed it was the first such international salute of courtesy Corea had ever received" (*New York Times* July 19, 1883).

When Lucius H. Foote, Envoy Extraordinary and Minister Plenipotentiary from the United States, arrived in Seoul, it was reported that the king "danced for joy" (McCune and Harrison 1951:3). Unlikely though this may be, first impressions between the American minister and the Korean king and his counselors seem to have been excellent. Foote's title placed him on equal footing with his colleagues in China and Japan. This, even more than the clause in the treaty recognizing Korea's independent status, was perceived as an indication of how the United States viewed Korea. Foote found the first officials to greet him "polite and intelligent, deprecating their own condition and seemingly well versed as to the conditions of other countries. At present they have the highest opinions of our country and its institutions" (U.S. Foreign Relations Papers 1883: 241, 245).

Korea's awareness of nations outside the East Asian world no doubt reflects information gathered on tributary missions to Peking. These missions served as an important channel to keep the Korean king abreast of world affairs even while Korea maintained its secluded stance.

Shortly after Foote's arrival the king sent a letter to President Arthur substantiating Foote's impressions. He described Foote as being "on excellent terms with us, honest and upright; and in the transaction of business at the capital he is always in accord with the views of my government" (McCune and Harrison 1951:3).

Not long after his royal welcome to Seoul, Foote discovered that the United States representative was regarded by the Korean authorities as the symbol of a beneficent power that would indisputably guarantee the integrity of the Korean nation. The United States, through its representative at Seoul, was often the mediating party in a most complicated situation.

Conflict between China and Japan escalated over their self-serving designs on Korea. Following America's successful treaty negotiations, other Western nations began maneuvering for position. The prospect of an independent Korea stimulated the diplomatic competition and the whole business centered on the United States Legation, thanks to Foote's successes and the United States desire for peace and friendly relations all around.

The State Department was well aware of the main diplomatic issues involved. The initial instructions given to Shufeldt and now reiterated to Foote showed an awareness of the problem. The difficulty for Foote, as it had been for Shufeldt, was that the State Department gave only the barest guidelines for carrying out the mandate. Foote was almost always required to use his own judgment. The State Department encouraged him to do so (McCune and Harrison 1951: 23).

King Kojong and his adherents viewed the Shufeldt treaty as a wedge to free Korea from Chinese domination. The arrival of Foote brought the

"King's progressives" so much hope that they set in motion a wholesale housecleaning of Chinese advisers. They based their hope and their house-cleaning on the premise that the United States would furnish capable advisers for the Korean Foreign Office and the army (McCune and Harrison 1951: 3).

Within two weeks of Foote's arrival in Seoul he observed that the Korean government "had little real strength," the country was "stagnant and impoverished," and in spite of many good people, years of subservience to "the dictation of China and Japan have created a degree of timidity" (McCune and Harrison 1951: 3).

Complex issues faced Foote. The reassertion of Chinese control over Korea, the widening Sino-Japanese rift, the slow Russian encroachment on the borders, the placement of strategic advisers with the Korean government—these were the major affairs of state at that point. In addition, Foote was concerned with maintaining a legation on a level commensurate with the status of the United States in Korea, though provided with insufficient funds to do so. All of these matters had to be handled by the man on the spot dependent entirely on his own judgment and sources of information.

One who figured prominently in keeping Foote aware of events and their implications was his naval aide, Ensign George C. Foulk. Because Foulk spoke Korean he was able to keep himself informed as well as help Foote. He also figured in the initial contacts with Koreans in America and later in the arrival of the missionaries seeking a beginning in Korea.

The king made continual requests to Foote for American advisers in foreign and military affairs (KHWM 10: 150). Repeatedly Foote requested his government for such men and repeatedly his requests were ignored. America's lack of response seems to have been more the result of indifference than an unwillingness to comply with the request. It is quite probable, however, that the reason the Korean king came to lean so heavily on Foote and Foulk, and later even invited the advice of missionaries, was the fact that the king somehow trusted Americans more than other foreigners living in his capital. When the officially requested advisers failed to appear, the king used those Americans at hand as substitutes.

Kojong was acutely aware of his need for help. Foote reported:

> Recognizing its weakness and ignorance of the usages of war or of treating international questions, and admitting its fear of both Japan and China, the government proclaims in open terms its wretched condition and seeks for aid from the representatives of the treaty powers now in Seoul.

The king patiently awaited the arrival of the requested American advisers as late as July 1885 (McCune and Harrison 1951: 11-15). Later even China and Japan joined the king in petitioning for American advisers, for they felt it would mitigate the growing Russian and English influences. In spite of the failure to send advisers, the presence of the United States was an influence for progress in Seoul prior to the coming of the first Protestant missionary.

If the failure of America to send advisers was the greatest problem of early Korean–American relations, the first Korean embassy to America may be termed the greatest success. Just as the treaty relations with Japan had opened the way for Koreans to visit Japan, so the establishment of relations between the United States and Korea made possible a mission of Koreans to America. The embassy to the United States arrived at San Francisco on September 2, 1883 (McCune and Harrison 1951: 32; *New York Times* August 31, September 3, 13, 17, 18, 19, 25, 26, 27, 28, October 13, November 8, 16, 1883). President Arthur sent Major General John M. Schofield, U.S. Army, to welcome them, along with representatives of the San Francisco Chamber of Commerce and the Board of Trade. Traveling east by train they stopped in Chicago September 12, stayed at the Palmer House, and then continued on to Washington (*New York Times* September 12, 1883: 1). Presidential appointees Lieutenant Mason and Ensign Foulk traveled with the group.

Foulk was included in the embassy party probably because of his ability to speak Korean, Japanese, and Chinese, which he studied while stationed in Japan, 1876–82. While functioning as interpreter for the party he doubtless built relationships with these leading Koreans. Thus in historical perspective Foulk emerges as an important influence in the formative period.

The party arrived in New York on the seventeenth, where they met the president and the secretary of state at 11 o'clock the next morning (*New York Times* September 19, 1883: 8). They visited as far north as Boston before retracing their steps back to Washington. During these visits they were shown the latest agricultural improvements, farm buildings, cotton manufacturing, carpet making, knitting mills, printing presses, pharmaceutical firms, and various public institutions. In New York they saw hospitals, a telegraph office, fire department, post office, Tiffany's, the docks, a sugar refinery, newspaper offices, the navy yard, and West Point.

Min Yong Ik, who headed the embassy, reflected on all he saw. "I was born in the dark; I went out into the light, and now I have returned into the dark again; I cannot as yet see my way clearly, but I hope to soon" (McCune and Harrison 1951: 7). Foote wrote in anticipation of the return of the embassy:

> The opportunity afforded them to examine not only the practical working of our system of government but our industries and to learn our sources of wealth and prosperity, as well as to come directly in contact with citizens and to experience so many acts of personal kindness, cannot but produce a marked and beneficial result upon this strange and interesting people.

Foote was convinced the Koreans would readily adopt advanced ideas and that this would lead to new growth out of which would come national prosperity and individual ameliorations (U.S. Foreign Relations Papers

1883: 125-26). These favorable first contacts established a climate of mutual understanding and appreciation which helped prepare the way for the coming of Protestant missionaries.

Initial Encounter: Koreans and American Protestants

As the Korean embassy traveled from San Francisco to Washington, the Reverend John F. Goucher, a Methodist from Baltimore, happened to be traveling east on the same train. After making himself known to the strangers, Goucher invited them to visit him when they came to the Baltimore–Washington area. A plan was already forming in his mind to encourage the expansion of Methodist mission work into Korea.

Goucher was no stranger to missions. In 1881 he helped meet financial needs for the Japanese work. He supported work in India for several years. Eventually he gave a quarter of a million dollars to mission projects.

In 1882 Goucher proposed the establishment of "an Anglo-Japanese university in Tokyo" and gave liberally in support of this new plan. His first gift was $5,000 toward the purchase of the property and then "$800 a year for five years toward the salary of a Japanese professor" (Methodist Annual Report 1881: 204; 1882: 142; Boorstin 1973: 563).

On November 6, 1883, less than two months after Goucher met and traveled with the Korean embassy, he wrote the Board of Missions of the Methodist Church offering $2,000 to "aid in commencing missionary work in Korea." He stated further, "In my judgment our church should enter that field with evangelistic, educational, and medical agencies at the earliest possible moment." Shortly after, he wrote again encouraging action and offering an additional $3,000 "to be used in purchasing a suitable site for our mission operations in Seoul." He stipulated the board should send "a competent, ordained missionary of experience and a medical missionary, both married" (November 1883 in Appenzeller Corr.).

Some indication of the influence Goucher had on the Board of Mission is evident in the application of Henry G. Appenzeller, student at Methodist Drew Theological Seminary, to go as the "ordained missionary" Goucher ordered for Korea. Though the authorities were ready to accept Appenzeller, corresponding secretary Reid had to convey word to the young applicant that "Brother Goucher feels we ought to have someone with experience in the mission field or at least considerable experience in the work of the church, building, diplomacy, etc." (November 20, 1884 in Appenzeller Corr.).

When Appenzeller went to the mission offices to be interviewed, Goucher was present with the bishop and Reid to conduct the questioning. Only when Reid, the bishop, and Goucher had agreed was Appenzeller accepted. The acceptance stated, "Bishop Fowler has just now come in and announces to me that he *and Brother Goucher* [emphasis added] have decided to appoint you missionary to Korea" (Reid December 20, 1884 in Appenzeller Corr.).

Goucher not only tried to stimulate the board but wrote to R. S. Maclay, director of Methodist work in Japan, as well. He suggested Maclay make a trip to Korea, "prospect the land, and locate the mission" (Ella Appenzeller 1892 in Appenzeller Corr.). In June 1884 the Maclays made the trip.

It would have been hard to find a man better qualified to make the preliminary survey of the Korean situation. The Maclays were appointed to the work in China in 1848, the second year of Methodist work there (Methodist Annual Report 1848). By 1855 Maclay was superintendent in China (Methodist Annual Report 1855). In 1872, at the general committee meeting in November, Maclay was commissioned as superintendent of the mission of the Methodist Episcopal Church in Japan (Methodist Annual Report 1872). Acknowledging Maclay's experience, the mission annual report announced, "This appointment has given the church great satisfaction and is the assurance of discreet and earnest administration in this new field which the society enters" (Methodist Annual Report 1872).

Maclay, his wife, interpreter, and cook arrived in Seoul on June 24, 1884, after a fifteen-hundred-mile trip from Yokohama. They were entertained at the residence of Minister Foote at the United States Legation before moving into a small house nearby, which Foote acquired for their stay (Maclay 1896a: 354).

Thus from the first contacts of missionaries with Korea a precedent was established of cooperation between them and the diplomats, as it had already been in other East Asian nations. America did not seek the right to propagate Christianity. Through its diplomats, however, it did press for religious toleration as well as an open door for the humanitarian aspects of nineteenth-century American Protestant mission endeavor.

In an article entitled, "A Fortnight in Seoul, Korea, 1884," Maclay showed not only excellent powers of description of the sights he saw, but perception of the domestic and international situation in Korea. He observed the depressed state of affairs there and wrote that interference of other nations had "depressed industry, discouraged enterprise, paralyzed progress, narrowed the sphere and aims of education, degraded labor, obstructed trade, and utterly demoralized the population" (1896a).

Reflecting on the significance of the Chemulpo treaty, Maclay gave much credit to Shufeldt, something which Americans in general did not do. Then recognizing its implications for the opening of missionary work, he said:

> This treaty with Korea was a trumpet call to immediate efforts for the evangelization of the Korean nation which Protestant churches, and in particular the Methodist Episcopal Church, could not suffer to pass unheeded [1896a: 357].

He also noted that the recent return of the embassy from America was discussed favorably in Korea.

Maclay took a letter with him to Korea, written in Japanese, which he forwarded to King Kojong, "a paper setting forth desires and objects of

Christian missionaries." It requested permission to begin a school and medical work but contained no "disguise as to the ultimate object being evangelization" (Methodist Annual Report 1884: 204). He was encouraged when "the king . . . returned a cordial acknowledgment with permission to open a work [sic] especially medical and school work. . . . "All of this was accomplished in a very short space of time, for only four days after the petition was given to the king, Maclay received the royal reply authorizing hospital and school work in Korea (Paik 1971: 82-83).

Maclay spent the rest of his time in Korea in a careful survey of the city and surrounding area. He also tried to "test in a quiet way the disposition of the people." He was looking for the best place to locate as well as the best method for beginning the work.

Beside the general survey, the Maclays called on representatives of Western powers, "who received us courteously and favored us with an expression of their views touching our proposed movement." Maclay did not fail to call on the Japanese minister, "who manifested much interest in our plans and very kindly offered to do everything in his power to assist us" (1896a: 358-59).

Maclay paid close attention to the attitudes of people. He found the Koreans at first "timid, suspicious, and unwilling to have any communication with us," but later they "began to approach us more openly." The sister-in-law of Maclay's interpreter came to discuss Christianity with him. A Korean officer living near the Maclays visited them and then offered to have Mrs. Maclay visit his own home. On another occasion the Maclays were visiting a resort area near Seoul. A government officer observed them, stopped outside his office building, and invited them in for a time of conversation about America and Korea.

Maclay found it difficult to leave Korea. He was so encouraged by "the royal permission to commence Christian work in Korea" that he wanted to stay and begin the work himself. In a colorful description of Korea from his missionary-eye view, he spoke of "this field, over whose broad acres I would have gladly scattered the seed of the kingdom, and into whose golden harvest it would have been an inexpressible joy to thrust in my sickle" (1896a: 359).

On July 15, Dr. and Mrs. Maclay boarded a ship in Pusan and returned to Japan. Maclay's assessment of his mission in Korea was enthusiastic. "The success of our appeal to the king when I . . . visited Korea . . . was complete. The royal permit to Christianity removed all legal obstacles, and the way was opened for Christian work in Korea" (1896b: 498).

Meanwhile, in the United States the *Christian Advocate* published a number of articles concerning conditions in Korea and urged the opening of the Korea field. *The Gospel in All Lands,* official publication of the Methodist Mission Board, also printed appeals for support of this new venture. The financial response to these appeals encouraged the board to feel the time was right for this new beginning (Paik 1971: 83).

After his return to Tokyo, Maclay began to receive letters from Korea.

Among these were notes of caution and concern. George C. Foulk, attaché of the United States Legation in Korea, wrote of the "discontent and feeling of insecurity among the people," and of "the increasing bitterness of the opposition to the progressive policy of the government." The rising frequency of robberies and other problems caused him concern "lest these untoward developments might prevent the immediate introduction of Christian work in Korea" (Maclay 1896b: 500).

To avoid creating unnecessary suspicion by the Korean court, Foote withdrew his previously offered help to purchase property for the Methodist mission. He assured Maclay, however, that property would surely be available when they came (Maclay 1896b: 500-1).

Undaunted, Maclay made further preparations for beginnings in Korea. First he hired a Korean gentleman living in Japan, Yi Su Jong (Paik 1971:78), to begin translation of materials for use in Korea. At the same time he admitted seven Korean students to the Anglo-Japanese College who had been sent by the Korean government to study "the English language and the principles of western civilization."

On September 8, 1884, Foote sent Maclay an encouraging message. "I have received renewed assurances from His Majesty that not only will no obstructions be thrown in your way but that you will be tacitly encouraged in founding a school and hospital in Seoul." On November 18, 1884, he assured the missionary, "If in coming here you carry out your intention as expressed to me of making haste slowly, I feel that the door will not be closed" (Maclay 1896 b:500).

Presbyterian and Methodist missionaries in Japan and China were aware of the possibilities of beginning work in Korea. They began writing to request their respective boards to take action and send men. Maclay was the first mission representative personally to survey the possibilities. A Presbyterian missionary to Japan, George W. Knox, planned a similar visit to Korea in November 1883, but mission business prevented him from going (Knox 1884:168). Both Knox and Maclay found their interest in Korea stimulated by contacts with Koreans living in Japan. They admitted Koreans to mission schools, taught them English, and preached to them. Impressed by Koreans, the missionaries encouraged their boards to begin work in the peninsular kingdom.

The letters to the Methodist and Presbyterian boards of mission from Knox and Maclay urging advance into Korea were published and stimulated strong interest in America. What Goucher did for the Methodists in providing funds for beginning was done for the Presbyterians by Daniel W. McWilliams, executor of the estate of Frederick Marquand. Significantly, Marquand's will stated the funds were "for the cause of education and the spread of the gospel of Jesus Christ, and in encouraging and aiding any good work either in our own country or in foreign lands" (McWilliams February 8, 1884 in Letters of Pres. Church).

McWilliams promised four payments totaling $5,000. This was considered adequate for the support of two missionaries. The letter offering the money was written February 8, 1884. By mid-April the Presbyterian board had not responded to this offering. Since McWilliams lived in Brooklyn and the Presbyterian board offices were in New York City, distance was not the reason for delay. Both boards, Presbyterian and Methodist, were concerned over uncertain political conditions in Korea and reports of persecution of Catholics. They questioned the advisability of beginning new work there.

Beginning in 1880 the *New York Times* carried background reports on Korea. Among the first things noted was Korea's inhospitable treatment of outsiders and disturbing political difficulties inside the country. In one report the *Times* noted "a marked but silent revolution has been going on in the country, penetrating even to the palace of the King" (*New York Times* June 11, 1880:2).

The turmoil in Korea was the result of conflicting political factions. Added to the domestic strife was the continuing struggle between China and Japan for influence over Korea. Significant to the coming of Protestant missionaries, the pro-Chinese party sought return to a seclusive and antiforeign stance. On the other hand, the pro-Japanese faction favored expanding Korea's relations with nations outside the East Asian world. C. I. Eugene Kim and Han Kyo Kim, in their study of this difficult period, speak of "the hopeless state of affairs in Korea and its inability as a nation to sail under its own steam in the troubled and strange waters of international politics" (1967). Although the forces favoring the opening of the country managed to prevail, the mood of uncertainty continued.

A report in 1882 after a revolt in Korea speaks of "the vigor and venom of the anti-foreign feeling" (*New York Times* August 23, 1882: 4). That this revolt had occurred after Shufeldt secured a treaty with Korea made it seem even more ominous.

However, of even greater weight in influencing Presbyterian board action was a report from George W. Knox, their representative in Japan. About the same time as the political troubles in 1882, Knox began sending periodic reports to *The Foreign Missionary,* a Presbyterian Board of Missions publication. Despite the potential danger Knox seemed anxious for the board to consider expanding into Korea. Following the signing of the treaty of Chemulpo, Knox wrote, "The United States are about to begin a new chapter of national intercourse in Corea" (1882–83: 210). Recognizing there might be some hesitation on the part of the board, he noted, "The whole subject surely deserves careful and prayerful consideration." He could not resist adding, "It seems as if we stood upon the threshold of a great opportunity" (1883-84: 17).

On April 26, Dr. Ellinwood, secretary of the Presbyterian board for the beginning years in Korea, wrote McWilliams accepting his offer (May 1, 1884 in Letters of Pres. Church). Within two months Allen wrote from China inquiring if the Presbyterian board would permit him to transfer to Korea.

Born in Delaware, Ohio, on April 23, 1858, Allen graduated from Ohio Wesleyan University in his home town in 1881. He went on to medical training at Miami Medical College, Oxford, Ohio, graduating in 1883. In the fall of that same year he arrived in China. Appointed to Peking, he and his wife arrived there in October 1883 (Harrington 1966).

Plagued with problems, it seemed as if the Allens might never succeed in their missionary career. Because of a self-confessed difficulty in getting along with others, they were snubbed by other missionaries on the outbound voyage. They lost some money and Mrs. Allen was ill. Unable to reach Peking, their final destination, they stopped in Nanking where they found the "people and the magistrates opposed to Christian efforts." After quarreling with a missionary colleague there, Allen, his biographer wrote, "stormed off to Shanghai completely miserable and thoroughly defiant" (Harrington 1966: 6).

Allen was a touchy, crochety man. His biographer called him thin-skinned, short-tempered, and unforgiving. Yet he was destined to pave the way for Protestant missions in Korea. One would have to conclude his move to Korea was more by default than design. Allen heard in China of the need for Western medical care by personnel in the various legations in Korea. When it appeared he was not finding a place for himself in China, Allen requested permission to go to Korea. As yet the Presbyterians had no work there so Allen's request called for careful consideration by the Presbyterian board.

The missionaries with whom he discussed the possibility generally agreed the move to Korea was a good opportunity. As physician to the legation Allen would have a certain immunity which would permit him access to the "native officials and upper classes" (June 9, 1884).

In July 1884 a combination of increasing interest in Korea by the board and the unexpected gift of money to open the work there caused the board to favor Allen's request for a transfer. The Allens left Shanghai September 14, and arrived in Chemulpo September 20, 1884. Two days later they were in Seoul, the first Protestant missionaries to take up residence there.

2

The First Protestants to Korea

Horace Allen's Foothold

Allen's arrival signaled the opening of Protestant missions in Korea. He was sent by the Presbyterian Board of Missions to China as a medical missionary. In Korea he made clear to American Minister Foote that he was a missionary and enlisted Foote's help in securing permission to begin medical work.

However, at the time of Allen's arrival the peninsula was not open to the preaching of the gospel. Political turmoil, domestic and international entanglements—all made a difficult period. It is not surprising, therefore, that the Presbyterian mission secretary, Ellinwood, wrote to Horace Allen that "much uncertainty hangs over the country." Later to Horace G. Underwood, who was soon to join Allen in Korea, Ellinwood wrote, "It seems to me everything is a little uncertain. The way is by no means open for mission work. You should be exceedingly cautious" (February 28, 1885; March 23, 1885; June 22, 1885 in Letters of Pres. Church). In his first report from Korea, Allen noted, "Missionaries are not at present allowed in the country though as physician to the legation I will not be molested while preparing the way for the work which will soon be begun" (October 1, 1884).

Foote's attitude toward Allen's coming gave evidence of the ambivalence caused by the doctor's presence. Allen wrote, "When he found that I was an M.D. and would not commence any preaching or like work till the proper time came for it, [he] gave me a most cordial welcome" (October 8, 1884).

Foote's reasons for welcoming Allen seemed both self-serving and altruistic. The presence of an American doctor was a comfort to the American minister and his wife as they served in this strange new post. At the same time, Foote saw an opportunity to enhance the American presence in Seoul through the services of a Western doctor.

Furthermore, Foote's early instructions from Secretary of State Frelinghuysen stated:

Believing as this government does, that the toleration of faiths is the true policy of all enlightened powers, this Department would be glad to see you extend your good offices within proper grounds and counsel the Coreans to treat all missionaries kindly [McCune and Harrison 1951: 35].

Foote also told Allen he had the private assurance of the king that soon, probably in the spring, mission schools and medical work would not only be allowed but quietly encouraged. The king was influenced by members of the Progressive party, who had studied at mission schools in Japan. Western education and medicine were deemed essential to prepare Korea for its place in world affairs. Thus the king was anxious to provide these benefits (McCune and Harrison 1951: 101-13).

As soon as Allen's entry was effected he began buying property. Adjacent to the United States Legation, the houses the doctor bought were those of a murdered nobleman who was believed to haunt his former home. So the American was able to buy relatively cheaply "ground and buildings enough for three families and ground enough besides for a school, hospital, and a chapel." Allen was convinced that Seoul was the proper place, "the only place of much missionary importance in the country and . . . the place from which all work must radiate."

The young doctor was assured by various Korean officials that people appreciated Western medical science. These officials were anxious to start a medical college. Urging the board to take action, Allen wrote, "Now is the time for you to get your hold. Secure the confidence of the people by a well organized and officially recognized medical work and everything else will follow without hindrance."

In summary Allen said, "There is a deal of hard work to be done in Korea, but by the grace of God we will take her, and hope to live to see the day when she shall be a Christian nation" (October 8, 1884).

In November, just two months after his arrival, Allen was anticipating progress. He asked the board to send another man in the spring. He expected to be able to speak the language by then, for although he had begun practicing medicine among the higher classes, he asserted, "I shall not work for the common people 'til I can talk to them" (October 8, 1884).

Presbyterian Board Secretary Ellinwood requested Foote's appraisal of the situation regarding mission work in Korea. In reply Foote reviewed his attempts to impress the king and Korean officials with the importance of allowing religious liberty. He stressed to them that religious teachers would encourage the people to "respect the rulers, obey the laws, and to be honest, truthful and moral." Foote reminded Ellinwood, "It is well understood that I belong to no religious sect," so his encouragement of religious liberty was more apt to be considered (October 8, 1884 in Letters of Pres. Church).

On December 4, 1884, just two months after Minister Foote's favorable assessment of the situation in Korea, a party celebrating the opening of the new Seoul post office was interrupted by an attack of a group of progressives.

Since 1882 these men sought to introduce Western ideas in Korea. Both in relations with Japan and most especially with the United States they found inspiration and encouragement.

Min Yong Ik, a young nephew of the queen, was known to be progressive when he headed the embassy to America. But upon his return to Korea his pro-Chinese family forced him to separate from the progressive cause. In the fall of 1884, the now reactionary prince encouraged a resurgence of Chinese presence in Korea, causing the Progressive party to despair. The December attack was their final effort to defeat the pro-Chinese group headed by Min.

Among those seriously wounded in the attack was Min (McCune and Harrison 1951: 101-13). Dr. Allen was called to tend him. Allen found Korean doctors preparing to fill Min's wounds with black wax. He prevented the application of this dubious remedy and instead used his Western skills to treat the young prince, who survived. Allen's medical credentials and the efficacy of Western medicine were thereby established at court. Shortly after the incident, Allen reported:

> The whole affair has been trying and expensive. But it has admitted me to the palace and given me a prominence I could not have gotten otherwise. Already the people know me and our work will not suffer from this event [December 8, 1884].

The significance of this early acceptance at the Korean court is hard to exaggerate. Only those of high rank were allowed to go to court. Others came only if summoned, and such a summons was rare. Allen had no official status. He was known to be a missionary. He was a foreigner practicing foreign medicine in a court steeped in Confucian ritual which favored Chinese herb medicine. The king did not lack for physicians.

King Kojong's favor strengthened Allen's position. Granting permission for Allen to reside in his capital as physician for the legations was one thing. To call on Allen, known to be a missionary and a foreigner, to treat such a noble personage in the court represented an extraordinary opportunity for the doctor.

Some difficulties remained. As a result of the December revolt many progressives either were killed or forced to flee from Korea. The year 1885 dawned with retrenched conservativism surrounding a progressive-minded king and queen, a discouragement to the beginnings of Protestant missionary activity for it had been under the progressives that approval was secured for the work to open. After the progressives were eliminated, the once wide open door was now only slightly ajar. What might have been years of smooth cooperation between government and missionary became a time of caution and concern. The king and queen still desired Western-style advance, but with the loss of the Progressive party the ruler's hands were tied.

Meanwhile, undaunted by the setback in the progressive cause, Horace

Allen continued using his position to gain a wider place for his work. On January 25, 1885, through the American Legation Allen petitioned Cho Pyung Ho, president of the Foreign Office, for permission to open a hospital which would introduce Western science and medical techniques to Korea. Allen promised that, if granted permission for the hospital, he could secure another doctor in six months. They would draw their salaries from "a benevolent society in America." An obvious reference to his own Presbyterian mission, he told the king of the organization's "hospitals in Peking, Tientsin, Shanghai, Canton, and other Chinese cities, two of which are furnished by Li Hung Chang" (January 25, 1885).

Allen's choice of words was deliberate. By referring to the Presbyterian mission as "a benevolent society in America," he avoided forcing the king officially to recognize Allen's missionary identity. By referring to China and Li Hung Chang, he sought to allay the fears of the pro-Chinese conservatives concerning the presence of a Western doctor and hospital in Seoul (February 4, 1885).

Allen had reason to expect his request for a hospital would be granted. Min Yong Ik was now fully recovered. Allen reported, "He appreciated my efforts, calls me his brother, asks me to travel with him and makes me promises and presents innumerable." Because of Min's recovery, Allen had increased stature with the court. "The king and queen have sent me kind messages of respect and confidence, also some presents of choice old Corean works of art." Allen appeared genuinely surprised by his success. "My professional efforts have been crowned with far greater success than my experience deserves. I have had some most astonishing recoveries and all I believe in answer to prayer." Thus the doctor-missionary viewed his work as the work of his hands, but the work of God as well (February 4, 1885).

Allen used many angles to elicit acceptance of his plan for a hospital. The sick would be cared for according to Western science and young men could be instructed in "western medical and sanitary science." Seoul could become like American cities in having one or more hospitals. Nor was he merely asking permission to build the hospital with his own mission's funds. He requested the king to provide an annual appropriation for running expenses to include lights, fires, men as assistants, nurses and coolies, food for charity patients, and $300 for drugs.

In one final psychological ploy Allen suggested a possible name. "His Corean Majesty's Hospital." Allen was sure "it would certainly be gratifying to His Majesty to see his people cared for properly in their distresses," while it would "undoubtedly still further endear the people to their monarch and elevate them in many ways" (January 25, 1885).

As the probable result of these many factors, Allen's request for a hospital was granted and a footing gained for American Protestant missionary activity in Korea. After a mere five months in Korea, Dr. Allen had a remarkable report to make in early February 1885. He was accepted at court by the king and queen as well as by most other officials in the capital. He was physician to the American Legation and received active support from Minister Foote and Attaché Foulk.

Besides his medical duties, Allen worked on the language. His teacher was "an intelligent old man" who studied the Scriptures in Chinese with "interest and approval." Allen picked up words in his contacts at court and then practiced them as he rode home in the sedan chair provided for him by Min (February 28, 1885).

It is small wonder his board wrote to commend Horace Allen on the progress of those crucial beginning months. He replied, "I am both pleased and astonished at your clear appreciation of my position here:"

Allen opened the royal hospital in April 1885, just seven months after his arrival in Korea. He termed it "a grand success" and said that both officials and common people showed interest in it.

Allen was forced to use caution in treating the king and queen.

It was their pleasure to have me come and treat them openly as I would a foreigner. But rules of etiquette are so strong it would excite the people and injure me. Therefore, they requested me to treat them through an officer who came daily with their symptoms. I prayed about it as usual and was successful [April 3, 1885].

Though Allen was steadily progressing in his medical work, the political situation was tenuous. Just a month before opening his hospital he spoke of Korea as "this unsettled country," and of the people as in "great anxiety" (March 5, 1885). The Korean court was still friendly to America, however, as evidenced in the king's repeated requests for American advisers. In an unprecedented meeting in the inner courts of the palace between the king and Foote, with just an interpreter present, His Majesty asked the American minister's advice on forthcoming treaties with England and Germany. Then he urged the United States government to encourage Russia and France to enter treaty relations with Korea.

The king candidly explained his reliance on America in dealing with other countries. "I fully understand the disinterested policy of the United States; and I wish always to rely especially upon the advice and assistance of your government" (McCune and Harrison 1951: 53-54).

In spite of King Kojong's pleas, by March 1885—nearly two years after his first request for advisers—Allen reported, "They have never come." In the meantime the king relied on Foote and his attaché, Foulk, for the kind of disinterested advice he needed (March 5, 1885).

The fact that all during the beginning years of Korean-American relations the king was actively seeking American advisers is an expression of the esteem with which he viewed America. Though suitable advisers were not sent by the United States government, the Americans on the scene played a surrogate role for the king. Thus diplomats Foote and Foulk, and Dr. Allen, were called upon to act in capacities beyond their official ones. Both formally and informally, officially and unofficially, the king continued to encourage, approve, recognize, and reward American efforts in his capital.

Underwood and the Appenzellers en Route

While these events were taking place, Korea appointees Horace G. Underwood for the Presbyterians and the Henry Appenzellers for the Methodists were heading for Japan. Horace Underwood arrived in Yokohama, Japan, on January 25, 1885. He decided to stay there for a time to meet the missionaries, observe their work, and to get acquainted with Koreans living in Japan. Almost immediately he began studying the Korean language while teaching English (January 26, 1885; February 16, 1885).

While in Japan, Underwood met Minister Foote, recently resigned from his position in Korea. Foote told him the way was open for mission schools but preaching was still prohibited. He gave the assessment that if the progressives had remained in positions of authority, "there is every evidence to prove that the work of missions would have received such an impetus that it would have been difficult to find men enough to do the work that would have been laid before them" (February 16, 1885).

The reassertion of the conservative faction immediately after the revolt of December 4, 1884, obviously affected proposed Methodist beginnings as well. On April 2, 1885, Foulk wrote to Maclay, "I regret to say that the present state of affairs in this country presents many features wholly unfavorable to your work." He feared things would only get worse.

It is true that some time ago the prospects of good work in all directions in Korea pointed to the springtime, but the later disturbances have dispelled all these. There is not one officer in the government now to whom the subject of your work could effectively be broached [1896b].

But the Methodist appointees had already arrived in Japan. Besides the Appenzellers there were Dr. William F. Scranton, his wife, and his mother, the first missionary of the Methodist Women's Foreign Missionary Society to Korea. On March 5, Maclay called a meeting of the Methodist missionaries in the Tokyo area. Together with those en route to Korea they met to discuss the situation, to plan for the remaining trip to Korea, and to talk about business procedures as well as plans for beginning the mission. The group also spent time praying for divine guidance and help in prosecuting the important work that lay ahead in Korea (Maclay 1896b: 500-1).

At Maclay's advice the Methodist missionaries divided. Scranton remained in Japan while, on March 23, the Appenzellers took the first steamer leaving for Korea.

The parallel lines of development in Methodist and Presbyterian plans for Korea converged when Methodist Appenzeller and Presbyterian Underwood boarded the same ship for the last part of their long journey. There was more to the parallel than just a geographical starting point, however. A pause in the chronology of beginnings will allow a look at the similar shaping forces in the lives of these Protestant pioneers in Korea.

The Shaping of the Pioneers

The names of Horace Allen, Horace Underwood, and Henry Appenzeller are synonymous with Protestant beginnings in Korea. They are the eponymic types. Through them comes understanding of the main patterns, the successful beginnings, and the peculiar characteristics of Korean Protestant Christianity.

The pioneers were shaped by home, church, and school. Allen often referred to himself as "American all through." His grand-uncle, Lyman Hall, signed the Declaration of Independence and another, Ethan Allen, was a Revolutionary War hero. Combined in his ancestry were New England influence and pioneering frontier spirit.

College intensified both his Americanism and his mission-oriented piety. Ohio Wesleyan is a small college in a small town. Yet in the colorful description of the school by Allen's biographer, "deep within there burned the spirit of the proselytizing cause, the flame of piety fanned by the breadth of human zeal." Many alumni responded to this "spirit" and their reports were regularly printed in the college paper (Harrington 1966).

Allen's colleague, Horace Underwood, was born in London, England, on July 19, 1859. His father was a scientist and inventor and a deeply committed Christian living in "constant looking for the coming of the Lord." He regularly spent Sunday afternoons with his children. After church was the time to review the preacher's sermon. Horace was deeply impressed by his father's piety and particularly his expectation that Christ would soon return to earth. The boy learned respect for the Scripture and memorized large portions of it at his father's request.

In 1872, when Horace was thirteen years old, the Underwoods moved to America and settled in New Durham, New Jersey. There they all joined the Dutch Reformed Church. Horace seemed to have felt called early to be a minister and missionary, in which course his father encouraged him. He was sent to a Christian preparatory school, studied Greek with his pastor, and spent much time in evangelistic work.

After finishing college at New York University in 1881, Horace went to the Dutch Reformed Theological Seminary at New Brunswick, New Jersey, graduating in 1884. Of seminary days his wife and biographer said:

The three years spent in New Brunswick were crowded to overflowing, pressed down, shaken together and running over with every form of evangelistic work which an active and intense young student could manage to crowd in between seminary duties [1918: 27].

The largest Dutch Reformed Church in New Brunswick at this time was pastored by a Dr. Easton, a man full of evangelistic zeal.

> On fire with a passion for souls, he soon had the staid and at one time rather cold, old church at white heat crowded to overflowing with continual revivals, wonderful conversions, early and late prayer meetings, after meetings and an awakened interest in all the neighboring churches [1918: 27-28].

Horace served unofficially as an assistant pastor and was deeply involved in all of these activities.

Underwood was also affected by the Salvation Army. The group arrived in New Brunswick while he was in seminary. He participated in their activities to such a degree that his family and faculty feared he might join them.

During the 1882–83 school year a returned missionary from Japan was studying at seminary. He wrote a paper on Korea and read it to a group of interested students. Underwood heard it and was impressed by the new opportunity, but believing he was called to India he tried to interest others in Korea. When no one responded to his urgings he began to wonder if he should be the one. His own church was not ready to send him, however, and his first inquiry to the Presbyterian board indicated they also were hesitant, owing to the uncertain political situation in Korea.

Underwood made a subsequent attempt to see if the Presbyterian board would reconsider and discovered a letter had already been sent to inform him of his acceptance. In December 1884 Underwood joined the Presbytery of New Jersey and soon thereafter began his trip to Korea (1918: 29).

In Japan Horace Underwood was greeted by veteran Presbyterian missionary J. C. Hepburn. Underwood began to observe mission work in Japan, study Korean with the refugees there, and plan the best time to enter Korea.

Probably the least well known of the three, Henry G. Appenzeller, was the pioneer for Methodism in Korea. He was born February 5, 1858, in Souderton, Pennsylvania (Griffis 1912). Originally from Switzerland, the first Appenzellers came to Pennsylvania in 1735. From the beginning they lived in a German community near Philadelphia. They were farmers, hard working, and faithful members of the Reformed Church.

Appenzeller's mother was a strong influence in his early life. Griffis, Appenzeller's biographer, asserted, "Heaven, home, mother were as one in Henry Appenzeller's thoughts. Each stood for a powerful influence yet were one, a trinity of spiritual forces" (1912: 60-61). Appenzeller's mother reared her children with strong devotion to the Bible and the Heidelberg Catechism. It was her custom to gather her three boys around her Sunday afternoons and read from the German Bible. "Devoted to the details of a well-ordered home, she ever held up before her children high ideals of life" (1912: 61-62).

When Appenzeller was twenty years old (1878) he entered Franklin and Marshall College. This institution, related to the Reformed Church, was located in Lancaster, Pennsylvania. Regarding his choice of Franklin and Marshall, he wrote:

College and Franklin and Marshall were father's choice and mine followed his. He advanced me $1,000.00 on my education which was my capital. When I became a Methodist, whatever may have been his disappointment, nothing was said against my course by him. He kept his counsel, if he had it, to himself [1901].

Like many such colleges in this part of the nineteenth century in America, Franklin and Marshall made a deep emphasis on personal piety of students and faculty. A sound education included both academic and religious concerns in wholesome balance (Dubbs 1903: 257, 272, 328-31).

Thus for Appenzeller the personal piety and religious devotion which characterized his home received fresh impetus and support. A year after he arrived in Korea he wrote to one of his professors at Franklin and Marshall, "What influence I have in molding the education of these Koreans will be in accordance with the broad liberal culture of my alma mater. I am a Methodist, but my love for my alma mater is warmer than ever" (August 20, 1886; May 9, 1887).

Information on the reasons for Appenzeller's change from the Reformed Church to Methodism is very sketchy. Griffis indicated that following his conversion Appenzeller associated more with the Methodists (1912: 70-71). He told of a period when Appenzeller was "in a state of mental restlessness," and was "spiritually dissatisfied with himself." He began attending the prayer and class meetings of the First Methodist Church in Lancaster. In addition, he made a careful study of the minutes of the Philadelphia Annual Conference of the Methodist Church. In his diary on April 16, Appenzeller noted, "I rejoice in the good work the church of my choice is doing." Shortly thereafter he wrote:

Today all my previous thoughts and debates about the change from the Reformed Church to the Methodist Church were ended, when I was taken in as a full member in the Methodist Church, which is the one of my choice. . . . This step is taken only after prayer and meditation for some time. Since my conversion October 6, 1867, I have been among the Methodists most of the time and feel more at home than I did in the Reformed Church and I feel it to be my duty to join the M.E. Church and what I did today I did with an eye single to the glory of God [1912: 70-71].

He was admitted as a member on April 20, 1879.

In a natural progression from home to normal school to college, Appenzeller, now a Methodist, sought his theological training at Methodist Drew Theological Seminary. When Appenzeller entered in 1882, Drew had been in existence only fifteen years. The academic environment at Drew provided theological education in an atmosphere of deep personal piety and corporate religious experience (Cunningham 1972: 8).

Henry Appenzeller's developing interest in becoming a missionary began at least during college days and perhaps earlier. On February 19, 1881, while a junior at Franklin and Marshall, he noted in his diary that he had just heard a sermon on missions and had been deeply moved by it. He recorded that he gave $2.50 in the offering and wished he could have given more. A week later he wrote, "The ambition of my life is to spend it entirely in the service of the Lord" (Griffis 1912:81).

While at Drew, Appenzeller and Wadsworth, his classmate and closest friend, shared a common interest in foreign missions. Wadsworth was interested in Korea, although at the time no society was working there. Appenzeller looked to Japan. Between them they possessed one book on each country and relished discussion about these distant places with fellow students in the lounge of Mead Hall (Griffis 1912: 81-82). Appenzeller often spent time talking with Wadsworth about his "call to the mission field." When he finally made his decision to be a missionary, he wrote of it to his future wife, Ella Dodge (Griffis 1912: 85-86). Ella was raised a Baptist and because of her devout faith was more than willing to accompany her future husband as he followed his "call."

It is not surprising that Appenzeller's interest in missionary service was encouraged during his time at Drew. Between 1873 and 1885, twenty-seven Drew graduates became missionaries. By 1938, 270 had gone into some type of missionary service. On April 9, 1880, twenty-two students from twelve seminaries met to call for a national interseminary alliance. The expressed purpose of the alliance was to alert prospective pastors and missionaries to their responsibilities in both home and foreign missions. The goal for the first convention was the "stimulating of a livelier missionary spirit among the students." It also sought to translate this spirit into some systematic program for the various cooperating seminaries (Shedd 1934: 216).

Both Appenzeller and Underwood participated in the Inter-Seminary Alliance when it met in Hartford, Connecticut, in 1883. Both of them spoke of that meeting as decisive in their call to Korea. Both of them felt a compelling sense of urgency to be where the "need" was greatest. Since Korea was so recently opened and seemed the newest opportunity for the spread of the gospel, they were inspired to respond.

Appenzeller's personal development with regard to missions in general and Korea in particular related closely to his friendship with Wadsworth. Some indication of this is gained from his deep sorrow when Wadsworth was unable to go to Korea. Though Appenzeller gave no reason for the change in

Wadsworth's plans, in a letter to Ella, September 10, 1884, he wrote, "I am hardly able to realize we [he and Wadsworth] are not to go together, but such is indeed the case. Much of the joy and pleasure I dreamed of is gone and I must seek consolation and strength from my kind heavenly Father."

Wadsworth apparently never became a missionary. Upon graduation from Drew he served various pastorates in New Jersey. Appenzeller and Wadsworth maintained correspondence, however, and other than those to family, letters to Wadsworth give the most intimate record of Appenzeller's view of Korea and his mission work there (March 15, 1885; May 2, 1885; July 18, 1885; February 19, 1886; April 2, 1886).

In the fall of 1884, Appenzeller began corresponding with the Methodist Board of Missions in New York. The three men with whom he had to deal were the secretary of the board, J. M. Reid, Reverend J. F. Goucher—whose money made possible the beginnings of the Korea mission—and Bishop Fowler, the bishop then in charge of mission activities.

In November, Henry had his first meeting at mission headquarters with these men. The questions they asked were routine: age, education, preaching experience, marital status, intended length of stay in Korea, and something of his religious experience. Appenzeller was impressed with the serious consideration being given to the beginnings in Korea. At the end of the day he wrote Ella, "I am free to confess that the awful responsibility of the work is weighing heavily upon me. I don't want to make a mistake, nor trust in my own strength, but lean wholly on the strong arm of God" (November 11, 1884).

Henry Appenzeller and Ella Dodge were married December 17, 1884, in the First Methodist Church, Lancaster, Pennsylvania. They then visited the Appenzeller homestead in Souderton. While they were there the long-awaited acceptance came from Dr. Reid.

> First allow me to extend heartiest congratulations to yourself and the lady which is by this time, I assume, your wife. The Lord abundantly bless both of you. Bishop Fowler has just now come in and announces to me that he and Brother Goucher have decided to appoint you missionary to Korea. I will be glad to have you report for duty any time [December 20, 1884 in Appenzeller Corr.].

There is no explanation why Goucher was now ready to approve the Appenzellers, but once they were accepted, things moved rapidly. In January Reid wrote them concerning ordination and appointment procedures, travel plans, and other details (January 2 and 15, 1885 in Appenzeller Corr.).

Henry G. Appenzeller preached his farewell sermon in the Souderton Reformed Church. "Into the edifice old friends, farmer folks, villagers and young people crowded to hear. All admired the handsome and stalwart minister." However, Griffis also reported, "Unable to peer into the future, mother, father, and relatives wondered that a man with such brilliant talents and flattering prospects at home should go out among the barbarians to bury himself" (1912: 88).

Griffis gave indication of the parents' feelings on that occasion. Of Henry's mother, "Mingled pride and sorrow . . . overflowed in her heart, voice, and eyes." Evident to all gathered there was "the mother delight she felt in her elect son, the scholar." Neither of the Appenzeller parents could "see any beauty to be desired in Korea." The Father, "having full confidence in his son . . . frankly grieving at his decision to work in the foreign land, became later reconciled to the idea." So limited was the world of most of those gathered that day that some "thought 'Appie' was throwing himself away" (1912: 88-89). Ella's parents did not attend this farewell service but it may be assumed they shared the mixed feelings of joy and sorrow.

At Drew the reaction to Henry's going was quite different. His training and preparation were for the preaching of the gospel. The report of Appenzeller's farewell at Drew gives evidence of this feeling:

The first break in the senior class, Drew Theological Seminary, was made January 14th by the departure of Rev. Henry G. Appenzeller who was appointed to the new mission field of Korea. That Wednesday morning service in the chapel will long be remembered. After an excellent sermon by one of the seniors from the text, "Behold the Lamb of God, etc. . . . ," the sacrament of the Lord's Supper was administered by the faculty. The solemn feeling took possession of all present, faculty, students, and friends. The spiritual emotion was too strong to be suppressed.

Tears came to many eyes. It was good to be there. The sacrament was followed by addresses from faculty, Brother J. H. Knowles, pastor of the Methodist Church (Episcopal) in Madison, and Brother Appenzeller who savoured faith in God for the triumph of the gospel in all lands.

Chapel exercises over, we accompanied our honored brother to the depot in Madison where we sang together, 'Blest Be the Tie That Binds." The train arrived and much interest was manifested by the passengers as they looked upon the long line of young men on the platform. The interest of the conductor was genuine for he held the train as long as possible while we sang a parting hymn, "Shall We Gather at the River," and now Brother Appenzeller and his wife are on their way . . . [*Christian Advocate,* California, February 25, 1885].

Griffis described the feeling that underlay the outward expressions that day. "The young men felt that 'Appie' was to be their representative as Christ's envoy in the new land afar" (1912: 98).

After traveling from New Jersey to California by train, Appenzeller was ordained in San Francisco February 2, 1885, by Bishop Fowler.

Henry and Ella sailed from San Francisco on February 3. When they arrived in Japan they received troublesome news from Korea: "Reports of all sorts, true, false, and exaggerated of affairs in the peninsular kingdom." The revolt of the previous December produced much unrest and confusion. Japan and China were still negotiating for position in Seoul.

After consultation with Dr. Maclay the Appenzellers began studying the Korean language and learning about mission work in Japan. After only a month of this it was decided that "the preacher and his wife" should go ahead "to spy out the land" (1901; June, 1885 in Appenzeller Corr.).

The trip was no pleasure cruise. Ella commented, "This sailing near shore in a fusty, musty, dirty, greasy tub of a boat is small fun" (March 31, 1885 in Appenzeller Corr.). When the ship dropped anchor in Pusan harbor on April 1, Henry wrote, "Mrs. A. very sick whole evening," and "I myself did not escape." On April 2 he and Ella went ashore and walked from the port into town for their first real look at Korea. Then they reboarded the ship and steamed on up the Yellow Sea to Chemulpo.

Because of extreme tides, ships could not come into port at Chemulpo. So the Appenzellers and Horace Underwood boarded a small "sampan" and rode it an hour to shore. Their luggage was handled "amidst incessant jabber and bawling in Japanese, Chinese, and Korean."

There were no bands playing and no drama attached to their arrival. Appenzeller reflected:

> The day was cloudy and dreary, the landing place desolate, the hotel Japanese, cold and cheerless, the food tasteless, the rooms without stoves, the beds, blankets and boards in perhaps equal division. The political outlook normal, that is, gloomy and foreboding. The United States representative in Seoul discouraged further procedure from the port. The captain of the United States man-of-war at Chemulpo waxed eloquent in his vociferations against going to the capital and possibly necessitating the landing of his men and exposing them to the wrath and violence of the Koreans. Residents at the place shook their heads disapprovingly at the rashness of the missionary in making his appearance so early and at such an inopportune time [April 7, 1885; January 21, 1901].

No doubt adding to her private concern was the secret Ella carried. She was two months pregnant with their first child.

They arrived at Chemulpo Easter Sunday, April 5, 1885. Henry, Ella, and Horace stepped onto the bare rocks of the Korean shore in a cold drizzly rain. Ella wrote, "I had never been so sick in my life." Yet her husband, sensing the historical significance of this moment, prayed, "May He who this day burst the bars of the tomb bring light and liberty to Korea" (1901; June, 1885 in Appenzeller Corr.; Griffis 1912: 98).

3

The Initial Protestant Introduction

Arrivals

Korea had seemed ready to welcome those who would bring "light and liberty" to her shores when R. S. Maclay visited in June 1884. He reported, "The success of our appeal to the king when I visited Korea was complete. The royal permit to Christianity removed all legal obstacles and the way was opened for Christian work in Korea" (1896b).

King Kojong and the Progressive party appeared to be in full control of the destiny of the nation. Step by step Korea was opening, moving toward a place in international world order. The major nations of the West had already recognized it as an independent country. The door that America was the first to open had now admitted others. The Koreans, the diplomats, and veteran missionary Maclay all felt this was the opportune time for the state of Protestant missions. To Maclay it seemed only fitting that Methodist Protestants should be the ones to do the job.

Maclay was not in Korea long enough to become aware that there was a powerful reactionary force in Korean politics that did not welcome the prospect of Western missionaries in the kingdom. The progressives were assured of the support of the king, the Japanese, and the Americans. The conservatives were supported by China.

The early months of 1885 saw much diplomatic maneuvering between China and Japan. Little of it had anything to do with Korea, but it added to the helpless confusion the king felt as he tried to keep his country on a steady course toward progress and development. "Unable to gauge the intentions of either Japan or China, the Koreans feared that a Sino-Japanese war might be fought on Korean soil" (Kim and Kim 1967: 54).

The negotiations between China and Japan produced agreement that both nations withdraw. This agreement, the treaty of Tientsin, engineered by Ito Hirobumi for Japan and Li Hung Chang for China, was not signed until April 18, 1885. So when the Appenzellers and Horace Underwood came to Korea on April 5, the outcome of the Sino-Japanese talks was still in doubt. It was clearly an inauspicious time for new ventures in the capital, as government life was at a standstill awaiting the outcome.

The treaty resulted in a decade "characterized by an unprecedently high degree of Chinese control of Korean affairs," and "an abrupt decline of Japanese influence in Korea" (Kim and Kim 1967: 58).

It may be argued that neither side, China or Japan, gained a victory. Both countries recognized the strategic importance of Korea but also wanted to avoid war. However, because the Korean progressives had either been killed or made to flee to Japan, with the withdrawal of Japanese troops China gradually reasserted its paramount status in Korea. In order to prevent this, Japan would have been forced to fight China on Korean soil, something it was not prepared to do at this point.

For the coming of Protestant missionaries, the tenuous situation nearly meant the closing of the door initially opened by the progressives. Without the continuing interest and power of the king, the door might have been shut tight.

At the time of the arrival of the Appenzellers and Underwood in Chemulpo, Horace Allen was almost ready to open his hospital. In spite of political intrigue, Allen's activities represented a pocket of peace and progress in a difficult world.

The reception accorded Underwood and the Appenzellers reflects this mixed set of circumstances. Because he came as a friend of the doctor, Horace Underwood was permitted to make his way immediately to Seoul, where he arrived April 6, 1885.

On April 9 Allen's hospital was officially opened. There were twenty patients on the first day. By the twenty-sixth of the same month Allen was performing four to six operations every morning and seeing as many as seventy patients in the afternoon. The numbers increased daily (Underwood April 26, 1885). The beginning of Allen's hospital was so precarious, however, that he worried about the sudden influx of missionaries.

Allen's fears related to the uncertain political situation in Korea as well as his desire to maintain a low profile regarding his missionary status. He felt, perhaps justifiably, that the sudden arrival of more missionaries would create an embarrassing situation both for the king and for the American Legation. Caution and courtesy prevailed in all dealings to this point and Allen was anxious that they continue to characterize relationships.

Foulk, the attaché, was extremely conscious of the dangers and hard pressed to keep his own position secure. With the successful opening of Allen's hospital he was congratulating himself on a mission well accomplished but, like Allen, he did not want a sudden invasion of new missionaries until things were more stabilized.

Maclay had requested Foulk's help in entertaining the Appenzellers, buying property, and other beginning matters. Allen reported, however, "Mr. Foulk is greatly worried. He says their coming just now will kill the hospital" (April 3, 1885).

When the Appenzellers arrived in Chemulpo, Allen wrote in his diary: "There is a Methodist man at Chemulpo, with a sick wife. I don't know what they will do. There is no place for them. We are full and Mr. Foulk insists he will not entertain them" (April 6, 1885). A few days later Allen recorded, "The M.E. family are still at Chemulpo." Allen would have kept them, he said, but since they requested help from the legation he could not or would not intervene (April 10, 1885).

Meanwhile, after meeting with the captain of the American ship *Ossippee*, stationed at Chemulpo, and the Japanese and British consuls resident there, the Appenzellers decided it was best to turn back to Japan for a time. Henry summed up his feelings: "When we gathered up all the information in reference to the political state in the country . . . we found that we had made a mistake in coming over at that time. The country was full of war and rumors of war" (May 2, 1885).

Perhaps carrying issues to an extreme, Allen wrote once more: "It has raised the question as to the propriety of missionaries coming and it has been decided against them. A very unfortunate thing as it was uncalled for and will hinder them in the future" (April 10, 1885). Underwood commented on the unnecessary complications regarding the Methodists' coming to Seoul: "Anybody can come here as long as they come as citizens of the United States and nothing else" (April 19, 1885).

Though the Appenzellers were the first Methodist family to arrive in Korea, they were not the first Methodists to live on the peninsula. Dr. Scranton, who came as far as Japan with the Appenzellers, waited in Japan with his wife and mother, fearing the time for entering Korea was not auspicious. In fact, after the Appenzellers left for Yokohama, Scranton tried to telegraph a message to them at Nagasaki. An American businessman, Townsend, just returned from Korea reported it unsafe, especially for ladies. Scranton decided then his wife and mother would wait until fall. Meanwhile he spent his time studying Korean by day and teaching English at night (April 23, 1885).

Scranton's reasons for not going to Korea with the Appenzellers included the political problems in Korea, the crowded steamer, and the fact that he found a teacher for Korean language in Japan. Finally, however, at the urging of Maclay, the doctor started for Korea. In Nagasaki he saw the Appenzellers on their return. They gave Scranton a negative report on conditions there. But Scranton decided, "In spite of their adverse criticism on Korea, I deemed it wisest to continue on my way to Korea where I could see and judge for myself concerning the state of affairs" (June 1, 1885).

Leaving his wife and mother behind in Japan, Dr. Scranton left for Korea April 28. He arrived in Chemulpo May 3, and the next day left for Seoul. The trip took Scranton from 7:00 A.M. to 3:00 P.M. riding in a "coolie chair." Along the way Scranton saw signs inviting all people to "His Majesty's hospital for treatment for all their bodily needs" (June 1, 1885).

From the beginning there were difficulties in relationships between Horace Allen and the other missionaries, Presbyterian and Methodist. Because Allen was established in his hospital and needed help, he invited Dr. Scranton to work with him until he could settle into his own ministries. On one hand, this invitation was innocent enough. Allen's hospital was not a mission hospital but the king's hospital. It would not therefore represent a capitulation by Methodist Scranton to Presbyterian Allen. Scranton did not look on Allen as the king's physician, however, or the physician to the legation, but as a missionary of the Presbyterian board. Thus, from Scranton's perspective, he would be joining forces with the Presbyterians by accepting Allen's invitation. Nor was Allen unaware of the threat to his own unique place if Scranton should start a rival hospital.

Scranton decided to accept Allen's invitation. Meanwhile Allen requested and received permission from the Foreign Office for Scranton to join him. Foulk strongly urged Scranton to accept the position. Accommodating himself to expediency, Scranton boarded with the Allens and began working in the new hospital (June 1, 1885).

Foulk was also trying to keep Scranton from starting a rival hospital. He feared it might embarrass the king. He told Allen, "The king and Koreans are proud of the existing hospital. If Scranton surpassed Allen's hospital, which he could easily do, it would embarrass the Koreans." Since this was the king's first venture in Korean-American cooperation, Foulk wanted to prevent anything that would cause His Majesty to lose face. Foulk further insinuated that representatives of the foreign powers would not allow it (Allen July 4, 1885).

Allen's hospital made rapid progress. It was a Korean-style building adapted by necessary renovations for use as a hospital. Already in May he had some fifty inpatients and was seeing an average of sixty outpatients each day. "The diseases presented are in great measure of the most horrible orders, and with their great numbers show the most deplorable sanitary wretchedness of the Corean people" (U.S. Foreign Relations Papers 1885: 347).

A report of the first year of the hospital's operation cited smallpox as the main disease from which the people suffered, causing over 50 percent of all deaths in Korea. Syphilis was prevalent and many suffered from malaria (First Annual Report of the Korean Government Hospital 1886).

Allen began a program of inoculation for smallpox. There is no evidence of resistance to this program. Underwood noted that before the coming of the missionary, smallpox was the "scourge of the country." After the missionary came he reported vaccination in nearly every village. Furthermore, Underwood wrote, in epidemics "the government has committed the making of sanitary rules to the mission physicians" (1908: 137).

Foulk commented on the attraction of Western medicine:

The readiness with which people of all classes, ages, and sexes patronize the hospital is very remarkable when it is considered how distrustful Orientals are in other countries accepting western medical treatment and the early stage of Corean development. It may be largely due to the fact that His Majesty and the members of the royal family repeatedly were treated by Allen [U.S. Foreign Relations Papers 1885: 347].

Allen reported 10,460 patients in the first year (First Annual Report 1886).

The beginning weeks of Scranton's residence in Seoul he spent getting acclimated to new surroundings. He was quite conscious of his role as Methodist "scout." He was not thinking only of the Appenzellers but about his own wife and mother. On June 1 he wrote his first report from Seoul. He assured mission headquarters that the Appenzellers could join him in a few months "as the doctor's (myself) friend, who is interested in the language." Scranton recognized this delay might not be acceptable to the board or the Appenzellers but he was convinced it was the wisest course. "I believe if the doctors are allowed to gain a good footing here in the eyes of the government and the people, all will progress well" (June 1, 1885).

Scranton, like Allen and Foulk, felt that a sudden influx of missionaries would prove disastrous to their purpose. A doctor possessed "the ready means of recommending himself to the people." All others who came would at first need to relate to the doctors, or the language and culture.

Shortly after Scranton settled in Seoul he wrote Appenzeller to say the couple could come to Chemulpo and begin there to study the "people, their customs, and language" (June 1, 1885). So by June the Appenzellers and the Scranton women were able to go to Korea.

Henry and Ella landed at Chemulpo for the second time on June 20. Scranton met his wife and mother and took them on to Seoul, but the Appenzellers stayed in the port city until July 29, when they also made their way to the capital city.

With the arrival of the Appenzellers in Seoul the pioneers were all on the scene. Some of the similarities have been noted. They shared common evangelical Protestant backgrounds both in their immediate families and in their liberal arts educations. They all responded to the challenge of Korea after an initial interest in other countries: Allen in China, Underwood in India, Appenzeller in Japan. The circumstances that drew their interest to Korea were diverse but all responded, feeling they would have the honor of establishing the particular expression of Protestant denominational Christianity which they represented.

The pioneers were all young. Underwood was twenty-six; Allen and Appenzeller, twenty-seven; and Scranton, twenty-nine. The boards in New York had placed tremendous responsibility on the shoulders of these men. Underwood and Appenzeller had had some pastoral experience and Allen had done his internship, but this was their first full-time position. No senior missionary waited to welcome them. No precedents had been established. The board secretaries had given them only the most general guidelines. Presbyterian Ellinwood wrote, "I cannot give you much information. You will have to feel your way" (April 2, 1885 in Letters to Pres. Church).

Secretary Reid was concerned for the Appenzellers also. "Very large discretion must necessarily be given you at this early period in the history of the Korean mission." He confessed to Appenzeller, "I do not know how God will open the work before you. . . . We must proceed with all carefulness regarding with very great consideration the laws of the country and the peculiar prejudices of the people" (Jan. 15, 1885 in Appenzeller Corr.).

Apart from what they were able to learn in their brief stay in Japan, the pioneers were forced to rely on their own assessment of the situation. The first weeks were spent assimilating impressions and tending to logistical matters. Where to live, what to eat, how to function, when to start and what to start, which was the priority need; these and other such questions consumed their energies.

In the best of times an influx of foreigners to the capital city of Korea would cause concern to the government. So the coming of Protestant missionaries at a time when the propagation of Christianity was proscribed was a matter calling for delicate handling by both the Koreans and the missionaries.

Presbyterian Beginnings

More than anything else, Horace Allen was worried that this invasion would upset the delicate balance of accommodation he had seen each side make. Mollendorf, a Russian adviser to the Korean Foreign Office, opposed Allen's hospital on the grounds that it was really a "proselytizing institution" (March 31, 1885). Reports went around that "no person would be treated unless promising to believe in Christ." Allen wrote, "This with the untimely arrival of a number of missionaries of sister denominations just as the hospital was to be opened made the prospect look very doubtful indeed" (June 1885).

Allen sought to allay any fears by suggesting Korean officials superintend his hospital. He asked the government to name it and Allen announced he would superintend only the medical aspect of things. The new Western hospital had caused the disbanding of a four-hundred-year-old dispensary employing one thousand persons, but since it was the king's wish, it was done. This was particularly significant because "the king knows that I am a missionary," Allen reported (June 1885). When the Progressive party was free to press its plans in 1884, such tolerance of Western medical missionaries would have been understandable. In 1885 it was remarkable.

By unofficial and informal means the king found ways to let the missionaries know he was aware of who they were and why they had come. In the world of complex interpersonal relationships which existed in Seoul, these informal contacts were extremely significant.

Two amusing examples of Allen's status at court give indication of the strange interplay of East and West at that time. On one occasion he was called to treat the king's mother. No man was permitted into the women's quarters of the palace and certainly none permitted to see the women there. She was well protected, as Allen wrote: "I did not see but a square inch of the old lady.

She was screened by curtains and I only saw a part of her wrist as her hand was completely bandaged excepting the place where I was to feel the pulse" (May 15, 1885).

Soon after Allen's hospital was in operation the king appointed five kisaengs (female entertainer-hostesses) to study medicine with Allen. These women normally played an important role in all social functions. They were carefully trained in the art of gracious hospitality and their presence at a banquet in court or the home of a nobleman was an absolute necessity. Only men attended these affairs and kisaengs were required to keep food and wine flowing. These women were also trained to sing, dance, and play musical instruments. It was a mark of wealth and social status for a man to have a number of kisaengs for his own social events.

Kisaengs were not prostitutes. It was not forbidden, however, for them to become concubines in the house of the man they served. In an obvious reference to this aspect of the kisaeng's role, Allen facetiously noted, "If presented for their ordinary use it would show that the Coreans have reason to think foreigners are gifted with extra brute endowments." Allen, however, decided the king had chosen them to be trained in Western medicine, for he wrote, "I intend at least to insist on that interpretation or their removal" (May 15, 1885).

Allen's efforts to maintain the delicate balance between quiet presence and aggressive seizure of opportunities were successful. In June 1885, just nine months after Allen's arrival, the king expressed to Foulk his desire to confer the degree of "Champan Mandarin" on the doctor. In Korean court protocol such a degree was necessary for free access to the palace. Without the degree a man was forbidden to enter the palace unless summoned, and in practice such summons seldom came.

With this rank Allen would immediately be identified in court circles and with the masses as a person of standing with the king. The rank would have required Allen to wear Korean clothes and adopt Korean customs, however, and Foulk felt it would not be proper for him to do so. So in a diplomatic sidestep the king conferred the rank on Allen's office at the hospital (June 22, 1885). This assured Allen the privileges of the office without requiring him to become Koreanized in dress and custom.

Allen's Presbyterian colleague, Horace Underwood, meanwhile spent most of his time in language study. Underwood studied with a "Romanist." At first this troubled the Protestant preacher but since the teacher was rated one of the best in the country, Underwood studied with him. In spite of his initial concern about Underwood's rashness, Allen now assessed him as "a good Christian, which is just what we doctors need" (June 22, 1885).

A second colleague for Allen arrived June 22, 1885. He was Dr. J. W. Heron. Back in November Allen requested the help of an additional man. Now, on the arrival of the new doctor and his wife, he saw their coming as "providential," maybe because the Herons seemed appreciative of his preliminary work. "They seem very grateful that it so happened that I got in here and have a place open for them and do not seem to blame me for having been first" (June 23, 1885).

By the end of June Dr. Heron was studying the language. "I cannot forget that my mission is to tell of the Great Physician not simply to exercise my own skill," Heron wrote. "I long to tell these people of the dear Saviour who died for them" (June 26, 1885 in Letters to Pres. Church).

Meanwhile medical work progressed. The five kisaengs were now "Lady medical students." They were learning English as well as medicine, and the queen took personal interest in the studies of these cultured ladies of the court.

The kisaengs-turned-medical-students wanted to visit Mrs. Allen, so the president of the Foreign Office, rather than wait for Mrs. Allen's real birthdate, simply chose a day to celebrate her "birthday." Then they secured Dr. Allen's permission. On the appointed day the president of the Foreign Office came with the girls, an orchestra from the palace, and "a lot of Corean food on native tables." The orchestra played in one room while the party ate in another. The girls sang songs "wishing Mrs. Allen to live a thousand years." More than just a party, Foulk told Allen, it represented an honor bestowed by the court (August 12, 1885).

Allen soon began projecting the need for medical men in Chemulpo and Pusan. Mission strategy in his mind required they occupy the ports with self-supporting missionaries who can be acquiring the language and becoming skillful physicians so that "when the way is open you can put a trained force right into the field" (August 12, 1885).

According to instruction from board headquarters, the Presbyterians organized in October. Allen was elected chairman; Heron, secretary; and Underwood, treasurer. Ellinwood seemed pleased with the progress they were making (Allen May 15, 1885; October 27, 1885; Ellinwood June 22, 1885 in Letters to Pres. Church).

The "progress" of the Presbyterian pioneers, however, was undermined early by difficult interpersonal relations. Most, if not all, of these difficulties centered around Horace Allen and his strange personality. His relations with Methodist Scranton were strained. Now there was growing unrest in Allen's own mission. Often his assessments of his colleagues were contradictory. On one hand, he considered Heron "a thoroughly trusty and good fellow." Yet again Allen found him "too good for the foreigners and not polite enough for either them or the Coreans" (August 12, 1885). Though at first these differences were petty and insignificant, they were to lead to serious problems for the Presbyterians.

In September Allen recommended Heron take mornings for language study. Heron took this to mean Allen did not want him in the hospital, so Heron not only continued going but went earlier and did Allen's work as well. Therefore Allen stayed home to study. Because the problem continued, Allen wrote to New York asking to be relieved of his post. He requested to be sent to Pusan "where I can be missionary in a quiet, inostentatious way and not be in danger of arousing the envy of every brother missionary who happens along." Or, Allen wrote, he would be willing to return to the States and "study missionary character from a distance" (September 2, 1885).

Allen felt Heron knew medicine better but could not deal with patients. He found Heron a "good man and pious," but "markedly sensitive and in the ordinary course of events I am continually treading on [his] toes." In spite of this adverse appraisal by Allen, Heron seemed happy with how things were going. He said, "We are delighted with our surroundings, the climate, the people, and are glad that our work for the Lord is here" (October 27, 1885; October 26, 1885 in Letters of Pres. Church).

Underwood seemed to grow in favor with Allen. In August he was approached by two or three Koreans who wanted to study Christianity and Underwood was anxious to begin his work. Uncharacteristically charitable, Allen reported of him in September, "Mr. Underwood will be the strong man of the field, he has gotten over his freshness, is a real Christian and already has the language so as to use it quite readily" (September 2, 1885).

By early summer 1885 there were ten pioneer missionaries in Seoul; five Presbyterian—the Allens, the Herons, and Horace Underwood; and five Methodist—the Appenzellers and the Scrantons.

Dr. Allen continued in the hospital. Heron assisted him some and studied Korean some, while Underwood spent most of his time studying language. In late August, Secretary Ellinwood wrote to the three Presbyterian families. He encouraged them to work together, reminded them they were making history, and emphasized the primary motivation for their presence by saying, "There is so much necessarily of the secular element in your work that we feel specially anxious that the great errand which we know you all have shall ever be kept foremost" (August 21, 1885 in Letters of Pres. Church).

This exhortation of Ellinwood's highlights again the tensions under which the pioneers continued to live in Korea. They wanted to be cautious enough to avoid trouble with Korean restrictions on their mission, yet aggressive enough to justify to the supporting constituency that they were doing missionary work.

Ellinwood assured them the church at home was deeply interested in them and praying for them.

> I know that you will realize the solemn responsibility laid upon you and will not fail to lay the foundation of the Corean mission in moral earnestness and consecration of purpose; thus you are safe in God's blessing and in the confidence of the church [August 21, 1885 in Letters of Pres. Church].

Methodist Beginnings

Of all the pioneers, perhaps Henry Appenzeller and his wife were most affected by the delicate political situation in Korea and its relation to the introduction of Protestant Christianity. After the excitement of arrival on Easter Sunday, dreary and rainy though it was, they found no welcome. There was no Methodist missionary already in Seoul with whom they could stay. They were told by Maclay to work through the American Legation and they tried to. But Foote was already gone and Foulk, fearing adverse consequences to the delicate balance of relationships in Seoul, refused to give them lodging at the legation. The United States warship stationed in Chemulpo, whose American flag Appenzeller rejoiced to see, was an indication of possible trouble that might require the evacuation of endangered American citizens. Certainly they would not encourage Appenzeller to go to Seoul while China and Japan were still in delicate negotiations to settle political tensions (Allen April 3, 1885; Appenzeller May 2, 1885).

None of this surprised Appenzeller. The Methodist Board Secretary in New York, J. M. Reid, anticipated difficulties on entering Korea. One possibility he suggested was for just the men to go first. They were to be sure the political climate was favorable to their coming before attempting to enter the country. In a clear statement of the situation, Reid summarized:

You are sent out with the understanding that the country is not formally open to Christianity. Only a little while ago Christianity was positively prohibited by law but we have had every assurance that medical work and the work of teaching would be highly acceptable to the Koreans. Therefore this will doubtless be your first work.

Though Reid was anxious to see the work "enlarge and spread," still he cautioned:

Proceed with all carefulness regarding with very great consideration the laws of the country and the peculiar prejudices of the people. I hope you will be able to lay in Korea the foundations for a temple to the true God [January 15, 1885 in Appenzeller Corr.].

Specifically for Henry Appenzeller and Korea, the board secretary stressed, "Your beginning will be largely on the line of teaching and medical work. There may be need of much diplomacy with the government officials" (October 17, 1884; December 20, 1884 in Appenzeller Corr). Because Appenzeller would travel to Korea by way of Japan, Secretary Reid instructed him to make his time in Japan a learning experience.

He was to study the modes of procedure in mission work and, if possible, also study the Korean language. Reid even thought it possible to secure the services of one of the Koreans studying in Japan to go with him to Korea and aid him. "Every moment of your time in Japan should be diligently employed in securing equipment for your future work." Finally he was to leave for Korea only when Maclay felt the time was right (January 15, 1885 in Appenzeller Corr.).

In the first report from Korea to Methodist board headquarters Appenzeller reflected on the difficulties they experienced entering the country. "Truly we have passed through many dangers both seen and unseen," summed up his feelings. Explaining their reasons for not staying in Korea in April he said, "Because of the political uncertainty, the danger of crippling the work by endeavoring to start it in troublous times, we reluctantly withdrew to Japan for a season." Now they were encouraged, however, that things were quiet and the troops were gone (July 2, 1885).

Finally on July 29, 1885, the Appenzellers made their way to Seoul. They had spent more than a month in Chemulpo, but since it was not their final destination they had kept most of their things packed to move to the capital (June 23, 1885).

In Seoul Henry Appenzeller was both impressed and appalled. Commenting on the difference between Japan, where other missionaries resided and were at the port to meet them, and Korea where there were none, he recorded:

> The path before us was untrodden by any other Protestant missionary save by Dr. Maclay last spring and by Dr. H. M. Allen a little later who now resides in Seoul. Truly we go to an unknown land. What is before us we know not save the usual experiences of those missionaries who first enter a new field. May the Holy Spirit grant us His guiding, protecting, and comforting power [March 31, 1885].

The Appenzellers located temporarily in a small house Dr. Scranton had been using as a pharmacy. Through the spring of 1886 they spent time purchasing houses and property and overseeing repairs necessary to make them livable (January 21, 1901). Their property was adjacent to the American Legation and the Presbyterians. Thus a small enclave was begun. Later this became a center of progressive activity as well as a refuge for the king in times of difficulty.

The house Appenzeller bought for $388 was formerly a nobleman's home. Measuring 32 feet by 12 feet, it seemed small to Henry and Ella but was larger than an average Korean home of that day (August 7, 1885). More was spent for repairs than for the original purchase but essentially the house was left in its Korean form. Appenzeller wrote his best friend, Wadsworth, that though they were living in a Korean-style house, he and Ella found it could be made quite comfortable (July 18, 1885).

Much of the time Henry was up from 5:30 A.M. and working until 7:00 P.M., supervising the work being done. Obviously chafing to get on with his "real" work, he wrote:

> When this work of preparation is over, the way will be open for other efforts. I suppose it is necessary to sharpen your instruments, erect the

scaffold, or dig away the rubbish to lay the cornerstone. The Lord help us not to spend all our time in this work to give some labor to the temple [April 2, 1886; May 14, 1886; April 22, 1886].

A year later, July 1886, Appenzeller reported completion of the first repairs. He reflected on the original dilapidated state of the property, feeling he and Dr. Scranton had made great progress in one year (July 1, 1886).

Along with living quarters, another concern was food. The new missionaries' first investigations in the bewildering Korean market turned up apricots, plums, peaches, apples and grapes, as well as cucumbers, onions, beans, melons, "poor" beef, chickens, and eggs. Appenzeller, with his farm background, paid special attention to the quality of meat. He learned cattle were worked to an advanced age and then turned over to the butcher. He and Ella were grateful for good teeth. Chickens were good "according to their youth." Other foods like flour, potatoes, butter, and "clothing down to shoestrings must be imported" (August 1885).

In order to introduce Protestant Christianity into Korea successfully, Henry Appenzeller was required first to learn to communicate with the citizens. His language study looked toward the day when he would be free to preach. With a private tutor Appenzeller studied five hours a day, three in the morning and two in the afternoon.

Since the Protestant pioneers in Korea were the first Americans to desire a systematic study of Korean, there were no language institutes, no English-Korean textbooks or dictionaries. The only tool was a French-Korean dictionary, which Roman Catholics had prepared in an earlier time, and it was hardly satisfactory.

Referring to his use of this French-Korean dictionary, Appenzeller wrote, "I am getting quite a knowledge of the French but it is hard work and slow." Appenzeller correctly surmised that grammar forms changed according to social relationships between the speakers. There were superiors, equals, and inferiors to be addressed and the form used depended on the level of person to whom he spoke.

Appenzeller started by using his Korean in the market. He said, "When they jabber at me I fall back on something that never fails you," and he gave the Korean equivalent of "I don't know." Then he continued, "It is amazing to see how crestfallen they become in a moment" (July 20, 1885).

Henry was bilingual before coming to Korea. German and English were easy for him, but Korean was another matter. "Some days this is exceedingly dull work and on others it is the reverse." In contending with a large number of customs opposing his American pattern, he wrote, "We are reminded we are on the other side of the globe where everything is done backwards" (November 4, 1885).

In the fall of 1885, Ensign Foulk informed the king of the Appenzellers' presence in Seoul and Henry's intention to engage in educational work.

Appenzeller said, "His Majesty graciously welcomed me and told our representative I could teach any pupils who might seek instruction" (1901).

Thus the Appenzellers moved from a rough beginning to recognition and encouragement by the king to begin teaching. Though he did not do so right away, Henry was assured of the direction he could take and of the king's prior approval when he did. A foothold was achieved. Through the long, cold months of the Korean winter, Appenzeller spent most of his time studying language in anticipation of spring and expansion of his work.

The pioneers arrived on Easter Sunday. By Christmas they were settled in the city. Their presence was acknowledged and encouraged. If the medical men had more actual work to do, the preachers needed time for language study. The preachers also received approval for their early teaching plans.

Major Issues

Most of the major issues relating to the successful introduction of Protestant Christianity during the beginning years had already become evident by this time.

The political situation has already been noted. A second issue during the beginning years was the Presbyterian-Methodist rivalry. The representatives of each mission arrived in Korea to work not only for Christ and his kingdom, but for their particular branch of Protestant Christianity. Their personal successes were not only theirs, not even solely for God and their high calling, but for the Methodists or the Presbyterians as well.

Horace Allen's request to transfer to Korea was to "pave the way for an aggressive native work." His voluminous correspondence to Mission Secretary Ellinwood gave evidence of his strong denominational loyalty.

Allen seems to have viewed himself as the paramount missionary in Korea. Because of his early medical success, his close relationship with the king and the foreign diplomatic community, Allen was somewhat justified in feeling superior to later arrivals. He expected them all to treat him with respect, request his favor, and be beholden to him.

Methodist Scranton, the third missionary to arrive in Seoul after Allen and Underwood, hesitated from the first to work with a Presbyterian doctor. As a Methodist he was interested in beginning Methodist work. Only after Foulk strongly urged him to work with Allen to avoid embarrassment to the Korean government did Scranton concede.

Allen liked Scranton at first. He described him as "a physician of good judgment and common sense." But his Presbyterian loyalty took over soon and he wrote, "It seems a pity to give our place after the fight we have had for it during the past winter." And in continuing vaccilation he swung back: "The coming of missionaries will be a great blessing be they of whatever denomination."

But Scranton "foolishly objected to playing second fiddle," a course Allen predicted would ruin him forever in Seoul. Since Scranton was temporarily lodging with the Allens, it made for difficult relations. Already Scranton was talking of buying property and erecting Western-style houses (May 15, 1885).

This bad feeling between Allen and Scranton no doubt had causes beyond professional and denominational jealousy. As early residents in the "Hermit Kingdom" they knew that every sign of acceptance, recognition, and progress was significant. The mission boards at home were anxious for news of the success of their pioneers, and the pioneers were equally anxious. For God, for their country, and for their churches success was a must. Every evidence of it was something to thank God for, and then to relate quickly to headquarters. Though in theory and after a few years in practice the pioneers would accept the unifying nature of the kingdom of God on earth, in the early months denominational particularity was a strong and at times abrasive factor.

Henry Appenzeller considered Methodist work in Korean began from his arrival in Chemulpo April 5, 1885. Though he was forced to withdraw to Japan he asserted, "The Methodist Church may rightfully be said to have entered Korea at this time as we left a part of our goods behind." Appenzeller's enthusiasm for his church caused him to write, "We went to Korea planning for the success of Methodism." He was conscious of pioneering.

> This working at the foundation does not show but it is very necessary. Gladly will I spend my life laying the foundation stones of our beloved church in Korea. . . . Methodism will flourish in the land of the morning calm [August 1885].

Strong denominational orientation made the missionaries keenly aware of every advantage gained, every recognition received, and made them zealous to see their denomination did not fall behind. The board secretaries in New York were equally jealous of place. Hearing from Allen of the coming of the Methodists and the details of their arrival, Ellinwood wrote he wished the Methodist brethren would "blow their trumpet a little more mildly and not scare an exclusive nation." A little later he said to Underwood, "I am afraid the Methodists may come into Korea and jeopardize matters. They are welcome if they will only be judicious." Obviously pleased that Presbyterians through Allen had been first to enter Korea, the secretary said of Methodists, "If they have been outrun in the occupation of the field, they should submit to it pleasantly" (May 25, 1885 in Letters of Pres. Church).

In a letter addressed to Allen, Underwood, and Heron shortly after they were all settled in Seoul, Ellinwood advised, "Keep clear of all partnerships with the representatives of their [Methodist] board." He added they "be courteous and kind toward all others but keep everything pretty close, and hold it firmly in your hands" (August 21, 1885 in Letters of Pres. Church).

A further issue between Allen and those missionaries who came after him was the degree of "real mission work" they were free to do. Scranton's hesitations in working with Allen included all of these factors. He wanted to start his own work for the Methodists. Further, he felt "Allen's hospital was not enough of a mission hospital." Foulk ordered Scranton to help Allen, but Allen reported, "He did as little as possible."

Because Allen's Presbyterian colleague Underwood was a preacher and not a doctor, Board Secretary Ellinwood took special care to caution him regarding his beginnings in Korea. Ellinwood wrote in March while Underwood was still in Japan: "It seems to me everything is a little uncertain except the matter of medical work. Dr. Allen has solved his problems, but this does not solve yours." In May after Underwood was in Korea, Ellinwood wrote again that it was "evident [you] cannot enter upon regular missionary work." The next month he again reiterated, the "way is by no means open for mission work. You should be exceedingly cautious." Ellinwood had heard of Underwood's wearing "an Oxford coat and a ministerial dress generally." Cautioning him not to continue such extreme practices, he suggested, "The true course for a Protestant American in a country where everything is yet so unsettled would be to throw off all ministerial dress and ministerial manner." Drawing upon a New Testament illustration to picture the beginnings of mission work, Ellinwood continued, "The mustard seed must grow for a time at least silently and invisibly in the earth" (March 23, 1885; May 25, 1885; June 22, 1885 in Letters of Pres. Church).

The peculiar problem faced by ordained missionaries whose central concern was preaching the gospel was quite different from that of medical missionaries. A doctor who was also a missionary was interested in more than just the practice of medicine. Medicine was a means to a larger end, what Heron called "introducing them to the Great Physician." But where evangelism was restricted or, as in Korea in 1885, prohibited, the doctor still had his medical practice to justify his presence. And since medicine was one of the more desirable aspects of Western civilization in Korean eyes, doctors were well accepted. Thus Allen, Scranton, and Heron received immediate acceptance by the king, the court, and the masses of Koreans who began coming to "His Majesty's Hospital."

For the preachers it was a different story. Underwood and Appenzeller's arrival marked the beginning step in an effort to evangelize Korea. They had come to preach. All their training had been for that, it was the great passion of their lives. And preaching should result in souls in darkness responding to the light, in sinners finding a Savior. To many, even among the doctors, this and this alone was real missionary work.

But preaching was prohibited. Thus both Underwood and Appenzeller came as friends of the doctors; Underwood with Allen, Appenzeller with Scranton. As the doctors' friends they could study language, fix up their houses, and teach. Underwood had a small amount of medical training and

Appenzeller had some training and experience as a teacher; so they both found measures of usefulness while they suffered under the restrictions.

Political uncertainty, denominational rivalry, adapting themselves to limitations on the propagation of the gospel—these were some of the larger issues in the period of beginnings. That all of them were either surmounted or adjusted for the accomplishing of their purposes is part of the story of success in this period.

4

A Hermit or a Seashell: Images of Korea Perceived, Created, and Reported

Early American Images of Korea

Much of the early missionary activity in Korea was influenced by images of Korea that the missionaries had formed before their arrival. Images influenced attitudes; attitudes influenced practice.

The earliest impression Americans had of Korea was symbolized best in its image as the "Hermit Kingdom." In part this related to the simple fact that few Americans knew anything about Korea prior to 1880. Even after that date it is unlikely that many Americans could accurately pinpoint Korea's place on the map, to say nothing of describing any of Korea's cultural distinctives.

The other side of the limited knowledge was the result of a deliberate policy of seclusion adopted by Korea as a means of national protection. Partly from fear of the unknown and partly from lack of any desire for international relations, Korea developed a policy of isolation that was only strengthened by hostile encounters with China, Japan, France, and the United States. These same nations, each in a different way and through factors both negative and positive, eventually helped lead Korea out of its seclusion and into the world family of nations.

The shaping of the image of Korea in the minds of Americans was taking place on two levels. The first was in official government circles where as early as 1866 American diplomats and naval officers were urging a try for a treaty with Korea.

Reasons given for this interest in Korea by Samuel Wells Williams, American chargé d'affaires in Peking, to Secretary of State William H. Seward were:

It will probably result in opening the last country in the world which still forbids Europeans to travel or settle in it, and establishing the dominant influence of Christian nations throughout the entire globe, if nothing worse to the independence of the Corean peninsula [U.S. Foreign Relations Papers 1866: 536-37].

The Naval Department seemed concerned only with securing a "treaty to regulate the treatment of shipwrecked seamen" (U.S. Foreign Relations Papers 1870: 333). Though the action of diplomats and naval men to interest their government in Korea was taking place during difficult years on the American domestic scene, because Secretary of State Seward was particularly anxious to expand America's presence in the Pacific, their urgings were not ignored.

The first American contacts with Korea were by accident. In March 1866 an American ship foundered near Pusan. The captain sought to purchase some food for the survivors but instead was given fruit, fish, and chickens without charge. The captain must have been greatly relieved at such generous treatment. Before regular contacts were established with Korea it had been reported "that its inhabitants were giants in stature, that their strength was herculean, their ferocity inferior only to that of the tiger." To be shipwrecked upon the shores of Korea was to be "subject to a terrible death by torture" (Cable 1938: 2; Choe 1972: 109-33).

In May of the same year another American ship, the *Surprise*, was wrecked near Pyongyang while sailing from Chefoo to the Ryukyus. Again the Koreans treated the men generously, giving them sumptuous food, locally grown tobacco, and medicines for the sick. Since the crew requested to be escorted to the Chinese border, they were given government hospitality all the way including guards, fresh clothes, excellent food, and often were entertained as honored guests by officials of the various towns they passed through on their way.

American diplomats in Peking were impressed by this Korean graciousness, reporting it to Secretary of State Seward in Washington. Thus when another American ship, the *General Sherman*, made plans to sail for Korea in July 1866, there was every expectation it would also be greeted with the same courtesy and fairness met by the other American vessels.

If Koreans had extended unusual courtesy to shipwrecked sailors, their treatment of the *Sherman* was quite different. Shipwrecked sailors obviously needed help and thus received it from the normally hospitable Koreans. However, when the *Sherman* entered Korea's Taedong River and sailed to within a few miles of Pyongyang, a totally different impression was given. The cargo contained "muskets, powder, and contraband"; the crew was a mixed lot, including an American captain, a Chinese crew, an English officer, and apparently a couple of blacks.

The ship was larger than any the Koreans had seen, causing a Yi Dynasty scribe to record, "It was larger than our largest ship as one could not see it all."

Of the blacks they noted, "The faces of two of those standing about were black and their eyes were like those of fierce wild animals" (Cable 1938: 17).

Most disturbing of all to the Koreans was the attitude manifested by the crew:

> The crafty and beast-like foreigners entered the inland waters of the Taedong, and in a few days came and anchored near the city without manifesting the least sign of fear. Their attitude was so threatening that one could not help but being terrified. Being strangers from a distant foreign country they should have approached us in a courteous and friendly manner if they intended to enter the city in the interests of trade. On the contrary, they acted in such a way as caused us to have great suspicion [Cable 1938: 20].

Some of the crew reportedly slept while the Korean party of inquiry was on board the *Sherman*. "The armed men and ship, the haughty attitudes, the high-handed demands made by the men were all such as to convince the Koreans that this was not just a shipwrecked vessel needing help" (Cable 1938: 50).

The government response was not surprising: "In order to preserve the honor and dignity of the Orient we must destroy the trespassing foreigners" (Cable 1938: 20). Cable's conclusion is no doubt an accurate assessment: "The presence of an alien armed force in the vicinity of a fortified and prohibited zone of another country without its permission, and with which the invading force had no treaty of any kind, was in itself a challenge to war" (Cable 1938: 86).

During this same year, 1866, there had been fresh waves of persecution of Catholic Christians in Korea. Along with thousands of Korean Catholics martyred for their faith in this year were some French priests. Because France sought always to protect its priests, the incident called for some retaliation by the French government (Kim and Chung 1963; Dallet 1874).

French Admiral Rose, commanding the French fleet in Asia, made a preliminary survey of approaches to Seoul in September 1866. He sailed past Kangwha Island, which guards the entrance to the Han River, and sailed up the Han close enough to the capital to be able to see the wall on North Mountain guarding Seoul from land attacks from the north. Having completed his "survey," Admiral Rose returned to Chefoo, with the Koreans never firing a shot, though they watched the expedition from forts along the river.

In Seoul reports of this French expedition produced havoc. The steamships with their thundering noise, columns of black smoke, and strange appearance compounded the natural consternation of the Koreans on finding foreign ships at the watery doorstep of the palace. Hulbert claims that nearly a quarter of the people in the capital fled, leaving their houses and goods (Hulbert 1962: 211; Choe 1972: 99-100).

Troops were alerted. The palace was placed under heavy guard. Money was allocated for the repair of ships. In spite of all these preparations, the Koreans maintained a policy of "wait and see." The "way of being kind to strangers had to be observed." The goals of the officials involved were to avoid provocative acts and to achieve the peaceful departure of the "little wretches" from Korea (Choe 1972: 99-100).

When Admiral Rose returned on October 11, he brought seven vessels and was ready for a full-scale naval blockade of Korea. Though the French initially succeeded in capturing Kangwha City, in November the Koreans managed to defeat them and the invaders hastily retreated to their home port in Chefoo.

These incidents involved two rivers: the Taedong in the north, the Han in the central part of Korea; two major cities: Pyongyang in the north, Seoul in the center; two Western nations: the United States in the north, the French in the capital. France considered the beheading of her missionaries an unforgivable national insult requiring proper retaliation. The Korean court felt threatened by the presence of foreigners who, in the name of a foreign religion, encouraged their converts to ignore centuries-old Korean tradition. It was even more provocative politically when these same converts made appeals for help to the pope in Rome and to France, thus inviting the possibility of armed retaliation.

Behind the French and United States attitudes was a show-of-force mentality. In a culture steeped in propriety and subtlety in interpersonal relations, such openly forceful initial contacts were acts of war. The extent of the Korean response was measured as much by the degree of insult to national honor as it was by the enormous strength and ferocity of the Koreans. To the French and Americans, however, it served to confirm the image already formed of a hostile hermit nation populated with vicious tiger hunters.

These tragic incidents only served to quicken the interest of American diplomats in Peking regarding Korea. Fortunately for later Korean-American relations, America had one of its most knowledgeable and able foreign-service officers serving on the embassy staff in China. George H. Seward, consul general in Shanghai from 1868, developed a growing interest in the establishment of relations with Korea. Several of the dispatches of 1868 which Seward sent to the State Department show the beginning attitudes that were to shape images of Korea in the department and also to create growing interest in treaty relations between America and Korea.

On April 24 Seward reported that four Koreans and a bishop of the "Romish Church" had come to Shanghai, sent by the Korean government "to make inquiries concerning the state of feeling existing toward Korea in regard to the alleged murder of French priests, and of the crew of the

American schooner *General Sherman*." He reported they were to ascertain whether or not it would be wise for the Korean government to send an embassy to America and Europe to explain these occurrences "and to make desired treaties of amity and commerce" (U.S. Foreign Relations Papers 1870: 336-39). Koreans felt the proposed embassy would be more favorably received in America than elsewhere and thus should be sent there first.

Seward noted it was satisfying, if true, that the Korean government was anxious to enter into treaties with Western powers. Further, he noted, "The empire is independent, although it sends complimentary tribute to Peking."

This was written eight years before the first treaty (the treaty of Kangwha with Japan) legally established Korean independence in Western eyes. It reflects, no doubt, Seward's discussion with Chinese officials regarding Chinese attitudes to Korea. He was also careful to urge that force, "or even the show of force," be avoided. Seward also knew this new relationship would have possible revolutionary consequences for Korea. Aware of Korea's traditional isolation, Seward nevertheless concluded that "Corea cannot hope to exclude foreigners much longer." He noted optimistically regarding Korea's view of America, "We are favorably known, and all the circumstances indicate that an attempt to open the country may best be made by us." Showing a more than superficial understanding of East Asian relationships with the West, he cautioned:

> Eastern states have a settled policy toward western powers which is dictated by fear that intercourse will result disastrously; they find occasion for this fear in the harsh lessons of the past, and in the actual condition of a considerable portion of their continent.

Noting that China and Japan were in a time of domestic turmoil he suggested these were "troubles which it would not be difficult to connect with the introduction of foreigners" (U.S. Foreign Relations Papers 1870: 336-39).

Actions aimed at attaining the desired treaty with Korea continued in the State Department. On April 4, 1870, Secretary of State Hamilton Fish requested Secretary of the Navy George M. Robeson to notify Admiral Rogers of the Asian fleet of the department's readiness to act. Since the *General Sherman* incident in 1866, the State Department had been studying the problem, for through the efforts of Shufeldt and Seward, interest grew.

Admiral Rogers was ordered to communicate with Mr. Low, United States minister in Peking. The two were to make plans to open negotiations with Korea. Secretary Fish instructed that the expedition should be "sufficiently formidable to make an impression upon the native authorities" and that Admiral Rogers should accompany it in person. The State Department maintained supervision of the mission rather than leaving it to the navy.

Rogers's fleet consisted of 5 ships, 85 guns, and 1,230 men. It dropped anchor off the Kangwha coast on May 30. They were shortly boarded by some lesser Korean officials inquiring as to the purpose of the mission. Minister Low indicated through a secretary that he could not deal with officials of inferior rank and through them he sent a message to Seoul asking an official of equal rank be sent to confer with him.

The Koreans had already received word through the Chinese of what the American desired, but they did not care to open relations with other countries. A policy for shipwrecked sailors was already established and they felt no need to meet the United States envoy to create another. The Korean court surmised that the *General Sherman* incident was at the bottom of this and thus had garrisoned the forts on Kangwha Island to deal with the Americans as they had the French.

As two boats from the fleet steamed up the channel for a tour of inspection, they were fired upon. Undamaged, they destroyed the Korean forts by return fire. Because the Han River channel from Kangwha Island to Seoul is the only approach to the capital by water, and because the Americans came in warships, the Koreans naturally assumed they were under attack.

On July 3, after destroying the fort on Kangwha as a token retaliation, Admiral Rogers and his fleet left Korean waters. Again, as with the French incident, the Koreans were left with the feeling of victory. Another expedition by Western powers was turned back and Korea renewed its isolation. Furthermore, the Americans were left with the feeling of hopelessness at further attempts to establish friendly relations with such an openly hostile nation.

When Japan succeeded in establishing Western-type treaty relations with Korea in 1876, Admiral Shufeldt once again took steps to make another try for America. He finally succeeded in May 1882.

Few of the impressions gained during these early years of Korean-American contact became public knowledge. Diplomats and naval officers conveyed information to authorities at the State Department and Navy headquarters. These impressions then may be said to have helped shape early policies relating to Korea.

While Shufeldt was negotiating to secure the treaty, on an unofficial level Americans were beginning to get their first glimpses of the "hermit." In June 1880 the *New York Times* began carrying articles on Korea. The report speaks of "the kingdom of Corea, of which so little is known, and the rulers of which have for so many centuries resisted every friendly approach to their coasts." It called Korea "the only country on the globe which is now closed to the rest of the world." In summary, Korea was unknown, unfriendly, unopened. Korea, the *Times* said, had been shut up "ever since the world began, as if it were one of the subdivisions of the moon's surface" (June 11, 1880: 2).

Much of the curiosity regarding Korea related to her assumed great natural resources. The *Times* thought it "teeming with the richest products known to this portion of the globe." Agricultural products, ginseng, and gold received special mention. Of the last it reported, "Gold is found everywhere all over the country both in quartz veins and in beds of streams" (June 11, 1880: 2).

In an interesting mix between awareness and anticipation, the *Times* exulted:

> As we are apt to magnify the greatness of the unknown, the prevailing belief throughout the civilized world has been that Corea is a land flowing with milk and honey, teeming with riches of all kinds, and filled with gorgeous palaces and cloud-capped towers, the like of which we have not seen since the days of Kublai Khan and his Oriental splendour. Cupidity has, therefore, been added to curiosity, and the commercial world is eager to break into this forbidden land, to ransack its rich storehouses, and to gape with wonder at its marvelous monuments [June 21, 1880: 4].

Fully recognizing that America's presence might not be all blessing, the *Times* continued:

> They have been tolerably happy with their stone huts, simple garb, few wants, and primitive manners; is it the fair thing for us to insist that they shall let us in with our brownstone fronts, tailors' bills, and the innumerable burdens which fashionable and civilized society impose upon the human race? [June 21, 1880:4].

In a summary statement of Korea's situation on the eve of the Shufeldt treaty, the *Times* recognized that probably the vast majority of Koreans just wanted to be left alone. But foreigners who wanted to open the country, even

> demand that they [Koreans] shall share with the blessings of the telegraph, railroads, newspapers, rifled cannon, etc. Whatever the end may be we pity the Coreans for the troublous times they are entering against their will [June 15, 1881: 4].

Much of the *Times* information and expectation was based on a reading and an acceptance of Ernest Oppert's *A Forbidden Land*. Since it was not originally written in English or intended for the American public, Oppert's book was not widely known. However, his report, though exaggerated in spots, was accepted by the *Times* as "the first connected and trustworthy account of the country" (1880).

Oppert dealt with expected topics: ancient history, social customs, religion, government, language, and geography. He reiterated a by now familiar theme in a new metaphor: "Corea has remained to us like a closed book, the contents of which we have yet to study" (1880: 3).

Oppert found Koreans "thoroughly honest, faithful, and good natured, and attach themselves with almost childlike confidence even to strangers and foreigners, when once they begin to trust in their sincerity." Because China and Japan were better known in the West, those who sought to describe Koreans often compared them to Chinese and Japanese. Thus Oppert said, "A comparison between Coreans and Chinese would only turn out in favor of the former" (1880: 129-31).

The favorable relations between America and Korea following the signing of the treaty of Chemulpo and the arrival of Minister Foote have already been noted. The reports of these events only served to confirm Americans in the step they had taken and in the obvious success thus realized. The success tended to reflect well on the Americans involved but also increased the favorable image of Koreans who so enthusiastically welcomed America's presence. The *Times* reported in detail envoy Foote's trip from Chemulpo to Seoul, noting the good-natured curiosity of "thousands of spectators" (July 19, 1883: 3).

This arrival signaled the "destroying [of] the last line of the chain which had hitherto securely closed her [Korea's] gates against the march of civilization and the advent of the ubiquitous foreigner" (*New York Times* July 19, 1883: 3).

The welcome receptions were covered in detail, even to noting the giggling court ladies, forbidden to attend the party, peeking through the cracks of the paneled screens secluding them from official goings-on.

In spite of the note of quaintness in all these reports, they built awareness, and Koreans who were previously unknown to Americans became more familiar and even friendly.

The visit of the Korean embassy to America was significant in building still more America's image of Korea. Invariably the first thing noticed about the Koreans was their dress. In Confucian Korea a man's rank dictated the size, length, color, shape, and quality of every piece of clothing he wore. Koreans could tell at a glance a man's social position and thus adopt the proper deference or dominance in the relationship. To uneducated Americans they were just "costumes."

One writer in a "Gossip from the Capital" column in the *New York Times* wrote of the stir the Koreans made in Japan en route to America: "Our visitors," he warned,

> will probably leave their loose garments, their fierce beards, and their horns and tom-toms at home; otherwise the American small boy is pretty sure to make their life here as uncongenial as Minister Foote finds his residence in Corea [September 3, 1883: 5].

Naturally, when the Koreans officially met President Arthur in New York they wore their ceremonial best out of deference to the American leader. One reporter's attempt to describe their clothes was, "Their dresses were similar to those worn by high priests in an opera chorus, only very much more gorgeous, and were surmounted by high sugar loaf hats, such as Alpine peasants are usually supposed to wear" (September 18, 1883: 5).

Perhaps even more startling to American curiosity was the greeting the embassy gave to President Arthur when they met him. All eight men of the embassy lined up in a row and, on a signal, did a full Korean bow, dropping first to their knees and then touching the floor with their foreheads. After the exchange of speeches the group backed away from the president and bowed once more before leaving his presence (*The Gospel in All Lands* 1885: 1-13).

Other than their "dresses," the reporter found "no peculiarities." He noted they "eat ordinary food in an ordinary manner." Further, he said, "In delicacy and tact they rival the Americans, extremely sensitive" (*New York Times* September 18, 1883: 5; September 26, 1883: 5).

For the most part these reports are surprisingly detailed, accurate, and appreciative. Whether from the knowledge that American Minister Foote had been so kindly received in Seoul or whether as the result of America's desire for friendly relations with Korea and thus the hospitable treatment, the embassy seemed to have confirmed all the more a feeling of mutual respect and admiration between Korea and America.

One other channel of influence in shaping America's image of Korea was a book first published in 1882 by William Elliot Griffis, *Corea, the Hermit Nation*. Through nine editions over thirty years it was the paramount source in English for information on Korea. Read by diplomat and missionary as well as college student and seminarian, it was *the* reference work on Korea.

Griffis's first contacts with East Asia were during the years 1866-70 when numbers of Japanese students attended Rutgers University. Griffis graduated from Rutgers in 1869 and was invited to go to Japan to help organize a Japanese Rutgers. During four years there Griffis became deeply involved in the study of Asian history. From the year of his return from Japan (1874) until his death in 1926, through books, articles, and lectures he was a builder of the image of Asia in the minds of his readers and hearers. At one time or another he lectured at Harvard University, Yale University, the University of Chicago, Cornell University, Rutgers University, Dartmouth College, Oberlin College, the University of Pennsylvania, Pennsylvania State University, and Union Theological Seminary in New York, from which he graduated in 1877.

While in Japan Griffis lived in a town he calls Fukui (possibly Fukuoka). On Japan's west coast, separated from Korea by only a few hundred miles, it was a point of cultural contact between Japan and Korea. Griffis said, "The whole region was eloquent of 'kin beyond the sea' " (1882: xii-xiii). Colorfully expanding on this theme, he said:

> Birds and animals, fruits and falcons, vegetables and trees, farmers' implements and the potter's wheel, names in geography and things in the arts, and doctrines and systems in religion were in some way connected with Corea [1882: xii-xiii].

Constantly intrigued by this evidence of Korea, Griffis reflected on the contrasts between Japan and Korea. Of the former he noted, "newly given up to schools of western science and languages"; contrasted to the latter he wondered, "Why should Corea be sealed and mysterious when Japan, once a hermit, had opened her doors and come out into the world's market place?" Griffis wrote for the general reader "to whom Corea 'suggests,' as an American lady said, 'no more than a sea-shell!' " (1882: xiii).

Though Griffis recognized his was not a personal experience of Korea, through Japanese translators and informers he compiled his history. Towering over the field, Griffis's work on Korea was the only major work in wide circulation until into the twentieth century. By then Hulbert (1905), Gale (1909), and Allen (1904; 1908) had joined him in the still difficult task of introducing Korea to the Western world. But the latecomers found little to criticize in the pioneer in the field.

In the preface to the 1885 edition of *Hermit Nation*, Griffis noted that Attaché Foulk was using his work as a field book. A personal copy had also been presented to the king of Korea.

Griffis's own description of his book is accurate. It is simply "a historical outline of the nation and a glimpse at the political and social life of the people." Griffis clearly emphasized the distinctive nature of Korea vis-à-vis China and Japan "in language, politics, and social customs, different from either."

Griffis obviously planned and prayed for the day when Korea would be "opened." "While the last of the hermit nations awaits some gallant Perry of the future, we may hope that the same brilliant path of progress on which the Sunrise Kingdom has entered, awaits the Land of Morning Calm" (1882: 10).

Griffis's work was recognized by the general student as an important source book. For the missionary it was must reading for the first quarter of American Protestant missionary endeavor in Korea. Coming as it did just as the Methodist and Presbyterian mission boards were increasingly aware of Korea's potential and the necessity of expanding their endeavor to include this hitherto closed country, *Corea, the Hermit Nation* provided vital information for decision-making by the boards as well as material they could reproduce in their publications to stimulate further interest in Korea.

Thus Griffis's work built a bridge from ignorance of the hostile hermit to knowledge and increased interest in Korea. Immediately on its publication it was reviewed by both the Methodist *The Gospel in All Lands*, and the Presbyterian *The Foreign Missionary*. Early articles on Korea in *The Gospel in All Lands* were compilations of quotations and photographs from Griffis and reports from missionaries in China and Japan. Many of the passages from Griffis were quoted without comment or credit.

It has been noted earlier that Appenzeller and his friend Wadsworth each owned a book on Japan and Korea. While the titles were not recorded anywhere, these must have been by Griffis. His *The Mikado's Empire* was published in 1876 and *The Hermit* in 1882. In the preface to the ninth edition of *Hermit* in 1910, Griffis noted it had "by their own unsought confessions, inspired not a few men and women to become devoted friends and teachers of the Corean people" (1910: v).

Supplementing Griffis's information in the period just prior to the arrival of the Protestant pioneers was the continual reporting from mission representatives in China and Japan. Unquestionably Maclay's reports influenced the Methodists.

George W. Knox of the Presbyterians also, like Maclay, stationed in Japan, wrote often regarding Korea. His reports were quoted in the Methodist *Gospel* as well as in his own Presbyterian *Foreign Missionary*.

The Missionary Image of Korea

From his arrival the Protestant pioneer in Korea was a man with a dual role; he was an agent of both propagation and propaganda. Propagation defined his role in Korea to Koreans while propaganda referred to his role in building America's image of Korea.

There are many facets to the missionary's role as image-maker (Fairbank 1969: 861-79; 1974: 1-23). Often in reporting and in real life he was a man in two worlds. He was both an observer and a participant. As the former he was an outsider, an onlooker, and he reported the different, the unusual, the strange. As participant he included himself in what was reported. In either role, observer or participant, he could be judgmental and critical or accepting and even complimentary.

Another two-sided tension was reflected in the gap between the ideal and the real. In one sense, the missionary saw at least superficially the way things were. Yet he wanted always to believe the best. His hope, his vision somehow transformed what he actually saw into what he projected as potential for the future. Thus the missionary within himself struggled often between despair and hope, between the actual and the desired, the need and the promise. Examples of this two-way tension in the missionary's perception and reporting are numerous. After the opening of his hospital, Allen noted the limitations of his situation. "No mission work is allowed in the country yet," but he anticipated "we will be doing aggressive work in the hospital by the time we are ready for it" (June 2, 1885).

Allen's colleague, Heron, wrote shortly after his arrival, "We are not doing active work but we are praying with all our might for the opening up of this country to the gospel." Yet in the same letter he wrote, "We feel convinced that by the time we can speak to them in their own language numbers will be anxious to learn" (Jan. 20, 1886 in Letters of Pres. Church).

Methodist Appenzeller shortly after his second arrival in Korea wrote back to Maclay in Japan, "Truly we have passed through many dangers both seen and unseen." Frankly overwhelmed at the enormity of the task confronting him, Appenzeller despaired, "What are we among so many thousands." Yet in the same letter he wrote, "We, however, feel encouraged because the Lord has given us a foothold" (August 1885).

It was not the missionary's own image of Korea and its people alone that mattered. A host of people at home were awaiting word from the missionary as a pioneer in this newly open country. The missionary now was the chief link between Korea and the American sending scene.

He was responsible first of all to his board. Board secretaries urged him to report often as there were many purposes to be served (Reid January 15, 1885 in Appenzeller Corr.; Ellinwood January 22, 1885 in Letters of Pres. Church). Most obvious was confirmation of safe arrival, locating, and beginning "the work." Progress and development were expected.

Beyond simply keeping board secretaries informed, the missionary and the board needed firsthand reports to inform and inspire the supporting constituency. Since the whole mission enterprise depended on voluntary prayerful and financial support of individuals, they needed to be convinced that the enterprise was indeed successful and thus worthy of continuing involvement. As the work expanded, new personnel were also needed and it was hoped articles in mission publications would be a means of challenge. Beyond the board and mission publications, the missionary wrote to family and friends.

Evidence exists that content and emphasis of the letter or report varied according to the audience addressed. If the missionary stressed a particular need, the picture would be painted one way; but if he wanted to assure of probable success, the hues would subtly change. If not actually altering facts, the missionary often choreographed the emphasis to create the desired effect. As a rule, reports to the board and for possible publication tended to be more matter-of-fact. It was to family and friends that the missionary spoke his mind and heart most freely.

An example of this difference in reporting comes from Appenzeller telling of his first attempt to enter Korea on April 5, 1885. To Maclay in Japan he wrote:

Some of us landed in Korea, April 5, and were not permitted to come to Seoul and because of the political uncertainty, the danger of crippling the work by endeavoring to start it in troublous times, we reluctantly withdrew to Japan for "a season" [August 1885].

To a member of his former church Appenzeller wrote regarding the same incident:

Mrs. Appenzeller and I went over to Korea but the country is full of wars and rumors of wars. Life and property are very insecure and our government officials advised us not to try to enter the country, so very reluctantly we came back to Japan. I am disappointed in this but hope it will be all for the best. I am anxious to tell the Koreans of Jesus but it is a very, very hard field and much grace and patience are needed to do effective work there [May 1, 1885].

To his Drew roommate, Appenzeller wrote, "I have met my first disappointment in my missionary life." Then at great length he described all the difficulties, summing it up thus: "I am greatly disappointed in having to retreat but I hope we can go back in the fall at least. You don't know how anxious I am to do just the right thing. It is on my mind night and day" (May 2, 1885).

Drawn from missionary letters and reports, a picture of Korea included descriptions both of places and of people. The first missionary to reside and report from Korea, Horace Allen, like all who came after him, had initially negative reactions to what he saw. Of Pusan, Korea's southeastern port city, Allen said, "It contains little of interest, being but a Japanese trading post" (October 1, 1884). Appenzeller's first view of Pusan tended to confirm Allen's. Sitting on deck anchored in Pusan harbor, Appenzeller tried to describe what he saw. Because the mud walls and thatched roofs of the then typical Korean homes blended with the earth, he had difficulty discerning the village. He wrote, "The houses seem more like large beehives than anything else" (April 2, 1885).

Both Allen and Appenzeller recognized that because of its close proximity to Seoul, Chemulpo was the more important port. Yet Allen noted that if one based an opinion of Korea on Chemulpo it would be limited to "rows of miserable, temporary huts, occupied by stevedores, the pack coolies, chair bearers, and other transient scum" (1889: 3-4). Appenzeller noted the "desolation and the dark places" (August 1885).

Seoul was the final destination. The road from Chemulpo to Seoul, though only thirty-five miles long, was not easily traversed in 1885. Allen described what all those who traveled this road felt. "The road overland is in most places but a mountainous path over which the sure-footed but vicious little Corean ponies carry passengers and merchandise in safety." The difficulty of the ride was relieved somewhat by "a constant change from mountain to valley, from pine clad heights to rich fields of rice, barley, millet, etc." (October 1, 1884).

Allen was disappointed, however, when coming over the last mountain ridge for his first glimpse of Seoul. He saw "a collection of hay stacks that have wintered out, while interspersed among the thatched roofs of the poor are seen the tiled roofs of the gentry, surrounded by their patch of green trees and grass." The city he found "pleasant or the reverse according to the weather and the streets" (October 1, 1884). Appenzeller found the streets of Seoul more filthy and narrow than anything he had seen before. He described the houses of the common people as "very primitive, built of mud, small, low, dirty, dingy" (August 1885).

One writer, noting the enormous gates through which Seoul was entered, wrote, "You may think that you are about to enter some grand city with stately abodes, but on passing through the gate you find only thatched cottages, very wide streets, and scarcely any trees." He concluded, "You are surprised that so grand a wall should be necessary to protect so insignificant a town" (*The Gospel in All Lands* 1885: 4).

Far more numerous than descriptions of the country are those of the people. In Korea only two weeks, Allen wrote to mission board secretary Ellinwood, his impressions of the people. He called them "exceedingly lazy and dirty," though middle and upper classes wore white robes and tall, black horsehair hats, giving at least a surface impression of cleanliness. The lower classes impressed him as "so dirty, lazy and such downright thieves, with all that they can never amount to much" (October 1, 1884).

Yet in the same letter Allen thanked Ellinwood for the honor of being sent to Korea and expressed confidence that "she [Korea] shall be a Christian nation."

With much of this assessment Appenzeller agreed. He saw the Koreans as "poor, lazy, and indifferent." He felt that idleness was the source of poverty and misery. Yet his negative impressions were tempered by favorable ones. He noted that "Koreans are an exceedingly quiet and peaceable people" (January 28, 1889).

In one report "the Korean is poor, lazy and indifferent." In another, "I found Koreans from highest to lowest, kind and courteous with a natural curiosity which was never intrusive." Thus the constant swing from good to bad. "This is delightful country," then, "barring its filth and idleness and poverty" (August 3, 1888).

In one long report that combines these opposite views, Appenzeller began, "They are poor as church mice, lazy as dogs, dirty as pigs, ravenous as wolves, and proud as hypocrites. They work little and rest much," And immediately in the next paragraph he said,

> But not withstanding all these bad habits and tendencies, there is much to be admired in them. They are reaching out for something they do not have. They feel or seem to feel the necessity for help in their endeavors to rise from their long sleep [1886].

In time a more balanced view prevailed. Early in the twentieth century, Horace Underwood, reflecting on his first twenty years in Korea, wrote, "How vague indeed were our first impressions. What strange things we expected to see . . . we expected to find a savage people, hostile to everything foreign, and of course, especially to the foreigner." Then he said, "We found a gentle, friendly, warm-hearted, open-handed, generous people who wanted almost wherever we went, to treat us as favored guests from afar" (1908: 371).

Besides letters written to the board and to family, the most important forum the missionary had in shaping the image of Korea was the mission magazine. They were read not only by interested persons of the missionary's denomination, but also in seminaries and colleges, discussed in preacher's meetings and missions conferences. All of this tended to confirm success and stimulate further interest in the endeavor. Ultimately the missionary on furlough would in most of these same forums present the case for continuing support of the work in "his country."

5

From Tenuous Beginnings to Established Presence

A hostile hermit or a seashell? Such were the confusing images in the minds and hearts of the pioneers as they arrived in Korea in late 1884 and 1885. The "hostile hermit" image suggested the very real possibility that the missionaries might suffer physical harm, even a martyr's death; a sobering thought for a young pioneer. Or was "seashell" the more accurate image with its suggestion of quiet beauty, passivity, even a bit of mystery? Certainly much about Korea was quaint, simple, pristine. But no one living in Seoul in 1885 could think of Korea as quiet and calm.

The pioneers all arrived by summer 1885. Their first concern was logistics. By care and courtesy they gained the right to live, to study language, to practice medicine, and to teach English. First acquaintances were favorable. The king seemed pleased with his hospital, his physician. He did not know the "teachers" quite as well, but if English was necessary to study medicine and American ways, then it was fortunate the doctors knew friends who could teach this strange new tongue.

The missionaries were comfortably housed, convinced that with care they could continue to function in this strange yet fascinating land. What remained was a slow, systematic building process. Scranton expressed the feeling of them all:

> I suppose during these trying days of overturning old customs and prejudices, and setting up new ones, it will be for many years to come in Korea, as it has been in Japan, until the leaven that is hidden shall pervade all parts of the country [*The Gospel in All Lands* 1885:329].

Building Begins (1886)

If 1885 saw the foundations laid, 1886 saw the building begin. The medical men were not as free to present the gospel to patients and staff as they would have liked, but they were working. The more patients they treated, the more old superstitions and hostilities regarding foreigners fell away. The knowledge among the citizens that the king and his advisers were taking medicine from the foreign doctors enhanced the status of the medicine and the men.

61

By association the preachers—Appenzeller and Underwood—gained their entrée. Early they too saw some beginnings of work which would later attach to their names. In fact, when later writers spoke of the pioneers, the two preachers were popularly referred to as the "first Protestant missionaries in Korea." That Allen arrived before Underwood for the Presbyterians and Scranton before Appenzeller for the Methodists became secondary in a view of mission that considered only preaching "real missionary work." To the preachers fell the difficult task of accommodating themselves to the limitations of the situation without compromising their ultimate goal.

Appenzeller's teaching began very simply. Among the buildings on the property he purchased there was an empty house that he adapted for classrooms, estimating it to be adequate for twenty or thirty students. Even during his preparation for opening the school he dreamed of growth and expansion, writing to his board in New York about the space at the top of the hill and how it could accommodate lecture halls and dormitories (December 13, 1886). The formal opening was June 8, 1886. On that day there were two students, one of whom promptly dropped out. But two others were added and the English lessons began. Books Appenzeller had ordered from America included English, geography, history, arithmetic, science, English and American literature, and art. By the end of 1886, the first six months of the school's existence, Appenzeller was teaching twenty-six Korean students and six Japanese.

The medical work of Dr. Scranton also expanded in 1886. At the first mission meeting of the year it was agreed to purchase property for the hospital. The reasons given were that Scranton had to treat patients in his own home, smallpox was in epidemic proportions in Seoul, the medical work had no place suitable for surgery, and the property in question was desirable for future expansion (Appenzeller, January 19, 1886).

Besides this the Methodist purchased land for the women's work and Appenzeller bought a piece he thought would some day be for his school. The prevailing mood of the mission was confidence. Appenzeller reported his own expectations: "Let schools be established and the Koreans see the difference between progression and stagnation and the grip of China will not be so strong." With enthusiasm he added, "I believe without posing as a prophet we will live to see the day when Korea will make even more wonderful strides toward civilization and Christianity than Japan" (July 1, 1886).

In a report at midyear 1886, Appenzeller revealed his satisfaction with their progress.

> The end of our first year in Korea finds us out of the woods. Dr. Scranton no longer mixes his medicine in an eight foot square room with a stone box for a table. His mother no longer lives in a paper house, or what is almost as bad. And I am permitted to meet my pupils, not in the dining room but in another especially fitted for the purpose.

In summary he said, "The way is opening, slowly to be sure, but steadily." There were Koreans asking about "the way of salvation." Others were inquiring about the difference between Protestants and Catholics. Though the beginning months were uncertain, now he could say, "We have plenty of work, enough to eat, enjoying a good health and thankful to God for calling us to this glorious work" (*The Gospel in All Lands* 1886:7).

Henry Appenzeller, the preacher, was studying language and teaching, but he was restless. "I may be pardoned for giving expression to the preference of preaching the gospel to continuous work in the lecture room," he wrote. He urged the board to send a teacher so he could give full time to preaching. "Our great and chief work is to *save souls* [emphasis his]. We want to take Korea for Jesus" (July 1, 1886).

If preaching was really the main work, no missionary could be content until he was free to preach. Hospitals and schools were started by the Korean pioneers not so much to civilize as simply to make use of the opportunity presented in order some day to gain the right to preach.

They felt free of duplicity, however, because their ultimate purpose had been made known to the king and his court. Maclay clearly indicated that Methodists planned ultimately for evangelization. Presbyterian Allen had been assured through Foote that the king would soon approve "mission schools and medical work." Allen's hospital was strictly a government affair so the emphasis on "mission" indicated a significant emphasis from the king (October 8, 1884).

Allen asserted, "Secure the confidence of the people by a well organized and officially recognized medical work and everything else will follow without hindrance." Difficulties arose among the pioneers regarding how much overt propagation to do at each juncture but all agreed on the ultimate goal.

Presbyterians

While the Methodists were reporting in confident terms, the Presbyterians were also seeing progress. Like the Methodists, their reports were balanced between caution and confidence. They were both avoiding precipitous action but were optimistic about possibilities. Heron expressed it best for the Presbyterians. "At present we are not doing active work but are praying with all our might for the opening up of this country to the Gospel." He believed when they learned the language the government would openly approve Christian missions (January 20, 1886 in Letters of Pres. Church).

Heron found "the people very friendly and most anxious to learn foreign ways and languages." The Herons had many Korean callers and Mrs. Heron always took the women on a tour of the house. The ladies were invariably curious about the organ, the sewing machine, and the kitchen furniture. Reflecting on these experiences, Heron wrote, "If we can make them thoroughly understand how we feel toward them we have gained a long step in aiding our work." He saw this as preparation for the day when "our word to them may win them when we tell them openly of Christ" (January 20, 1886).

Meanwhile they continued to work on their "words." Underwood made extraordinary progress, though the study of Korean was never easy. Heron wrote that grammar construction and pronunciation were extremely difficult. The problem was compounded, he said, because there were "no Koreans who understand sufficient English grammar to render one sure that mood or tenses or even parts of speech at all correspond or that an exact meaning is given to any word." He summed up the feeling of his colleagues, both Presbyterian and Methodist, when he said that "next to having one's soul on fire with enthusiasm for saving souls is a thorough knowledge of the language" (February 1, 1886 in Letters of Pres. Church).

Allen's hospital work continued to grow. He and Heron avoided surgery of which they were unsure so as not to cast discredit on Western medicine. But minor operations they did by the hundreds and the dispensary attracted patients from all over the country (Feb. 12, 1886 in Letters of Pres. Church).

Though Allen was defensively protective of the work he was doing in the king's hospital, Heron and others were frustrated by the prohibition against overt evangelization. Heron thought the day might come when they would want to turn Allen's hospital over to the Koreans and start a more openly mission-oriented one. In such a hospital, Heron envisioned, "we may not only help the suffering body but try to say some word that will bring them to Christ" (February 1, 1886 in Letters of Pres. Church).

Heron is but echoing Appenzeller's earlier frustration regarding the school as a means of evangelization. Heron could not satisfy himself that practicing medicine of itself constituted mission work. Medical work for him was to be a means. Allen seemed overly cautious in Heron's opinion, for Heron wanted to introduce his patients to Christ.

For the present, however, Heron was willing to bide his time as he saw that he and his colleagues were gradually winning the respect of the government. In connection with the hospital, they started a school of medicine, adding more students to the five kisaengs sent from court.

In the continuing competition between Presbyterians and Methodists, 1886 saw a race to be first to bring a woman doctor to Korea. Recognizing the enormous influence such a woman could have on the powerful queen and her court ladies, both missions urged their boards to respond quickly. Each longed to be first in filling this prestigious opportunity. Underwood wrote, "I think that a little rivalry is not out of place and I do want our mission to keep ahead" (February 17, 1886).

Appenzeller urged his board to send a woman physician as he felt the Methodists were working "at great disadvantage" to "our sister society." Aware of the success of Dr. Allen's work and his closer relations with the king, queen, and other high officials, Appenzeller wanted the Methodists to be first with the woman doctor. "I should be very sorry to lose this opportunity" (April 2, 1886).

Allen projected this plan one step further. Since Underwood was still a bachelor the doctor felt, "If one [woman doctor] could come out soon and marry Mr. Underwood our prospects here would be grand indeed." Allen heard the Methodists were announcing they had a woman doctor on the way. But in conversation with the senior Mrs. Scranton he tricked her into admitting they were only hoping to get one but as yet were unsuccessful. So he wrote somewhat facetiously, "If you are quick we may convert the Wicked Queen of Korea. Otherwise the Methodists may have that pleasure" (March 14, 1886). Heron agreed to the strategic place a woman physician would have. He felt such access to the queen would "advance many years the cause of Christianity in this land." In July the Presbyterians won the race to have the first woman "doctor" in Seoul. Though she was only a nurse, Allen reported that "Dr." Ellers had arrived (July 9, 1886).

Regarding his efforts to get Annie Ellers in for her first visit to the queen, Allen wrote that the court physicians did all they could to oppose it. When the queen continued sick she sent for medicine. Allen refused to send it unless Miss Ellers first examined Her Majesty. Finally the court physicians were overruled and Annie gained her entrée (August 20, 1886). By mid-August she had been to see the queen six times. She wrote that the queen was "not very sick but likes to have me come."

On her first visit to the queen Miss Ellers went with Dr. Allen. When they were shown into the room she saw a lady and two men seated on a sofa while everyone else stood. Annie was introduced to Her Majesty, then was invited to sit by her and examine her. Only later did she learn that the two men seated by the queen were the king and crown prince.

Each time after that when Miss Ellers called at the palace the same three were there to meet her. She wrote that on conclusion of her third visit they all rose and said goodbye to her in English. This happened on each succeeding visit. The king had practiced counting in English and she reported that every time he did this for her he was "amused as any little child at home" (August 18, 1886 in Letters of Pres. Church).

Allen happily complained that the queen kept them coming back even though she was recovered. He said, "The queen has taken quite a fancy to 'Dr.' Ellers and keeps her by her side a long time."

Miss Ellers wrote that the queen was anxious for her to like Korea. "She hoped I would like it well enough to stay here a long time." The queen provided Miss Ellers with "a very fine six-man chair in which I ride when calling on her" (August 18, 1886 in Letters of Pres. Church).

In October Allen reported, "She is treated with unheard-of respect by the whole royal family." Then in detail he wrote,

Miss Dr. Ellers and myself are receiving the praise of the whole kingdom for the cure of the queen whom the native physicians had given up.
In fact I think they overdo it. Even low people come to render their

tribute. We are often called to the palace now even though the royal family are not sick. His Majesty asks me concerning the news, purchase of ships, etc., and the queen talks with Miss Ellers who is learning Korean fast. The queen seems really fond of her company irrespective of her professional character. It is simply astounding the way she is allowed to sit when all other foreigners must stand and the royal family squat around her on ottomans and try to teach her Korean while she teaches them English and I wait in another room.

In addition, Miss Ellers was given official rank equal to that of the wife of Min Yong Ik and second to Min's mother, the highest woman outside the royal family. Allen observed, "It is pretty rapid work for Miss Ellers to do in three months" (August 20, 1886; October 28, 1886).

Another Presbyterian event of 1886 was the establishment of an orphanage. Early in the year Underwood was struggling with the next step to be taken in his work. He felt the government would approve some type of school work, yet he felt it would be impossible to compete with government schools, which charged no tuition and gave students food, clothing, and pocket money. His proposal was to take in "homeless and destitute children as orphans and those of illegitimate birth." These he could care for and see they were "trained up in a right way and taught to love the Savior" (January 20, 1886).

Underwood saw the orphanage as only a beginning from which other work would grow. A day school could be connected to the orphanage to teach poorer children to read in their own language, to learn English, arithmetic, geography, and history. Ever aware of government prohibition against the propagation of Christianity, he wrote, "Although we might not at first be allowed to teach Christianity, we could be gradually teaching them things that would prepare their minds to receive the truth of the gospel" (January 31, 1886).

In conflicting views as to the best approach, Dr. Allen felt the orphanage-school should be a government affair like his hospital, while Underwood and Heron both wanted to keep it in mission hands. It was better, in their view, to limit the evangelistic concerns for a time, yet keep the school related to the mission rather than allow it to be a government school and lose all control. Foulk supported Underwood and Heron in this view. He agreed "a school was different from a hospital" because later they would want "to do more direct Christian work there than could ever be done in a government hospital."

Allen capitulated and signed the request with Heron and Underwood that was submitted through Foulk to the president of the Foreign Office. The reply must have gratified them all. "What on earth is more worthy of the consideration of this government than this proposition, a plan which has not been thought of before. Who, hearing of it would not approve of it?" Not only was it approved but the president of the Foreign Office encouraged them to ask if they needed advice and counsel from the Korean government (Underwood February 13, 1886; Foulk February 15, 1886).

In spite of this favorable response from the government, Horace Allen still had misgivings about the orphanage concept. His concerns reflected the dilemma of missionaries in a country prohibiting propagation of the faith. Allen preferred an indirect approach. If they introduced "institutions of modern civilization," it would be better than trying for "a feeble proselytizing concern." Allen's philosophy was summed up when he wrote, "Christianity always goes with the missionary even if he be serving an institution where if not proscribed it is taught with more or less secrecy" (February 18, 1886). But Heron and Underwood felt Allen's approach was too indirect and wanted to be more openly evangelistic.

As 1886 ended, the quarrel still was not settled, but the year was not a loss for the Presbyterians. Like the Methodists, they saw several areas of work either begun or expanded. And they saw their first Korean convert.

Mr. No Toh Sa (Paik 1971:136-37) first heard about Christianity from a Chinese book opposing it. Since it was a "foreign religion" he came to foreigners to learn more about it. While in Dr. Allen's home he saw the gospels of Mark and Luke in Chinese and stole them to read. Then he took his questions to Underwood. After some discussion together Underwood gave him commentaries on the gospels plus a couple of tracts and a simple book of doctrine, all in Chinese. The man began attending the English Sunday services held for the missionaries. One Sunday after a Communion service he approached Underwood about baptism. Underwood wrote, "I had never said anything to him on this point and it is a conclusion he has arrived at of his own accord."

After quizzing him in a catechetical fashion on various points of doctrine, Underwood warned Mr. No that "as yet he was going contrary to the laws of his country and that if he took this step there should be no turning back and he seems to have thoroughly considered the whole subject."

If there was concern on the part of the missionaries at the possibility of adverse publicity resulting from this baptism, it is not evident in their letters. Even Ellinwood, who repeatedly urged caution, wrote to Allen, "Rejoice with him [Underwood] in the encouragement he receives in his direct Christian work." To Underwood Ellinwood wrote that this baptism was the "first dawn of spiritual success." He rejoiced with him in this "first streak of dawn" (September 9, 1886 in Letters of Pres. Church).

Naturally Underwood and his colleagues were elated over this man's decision. Underwood called him the "first fruits of our work," and remarked that he came in spite of there being no material yet translated into Korean and when Underwood could still use only a few words. In the same report Underwood indicated there were one or two others studying, one of them in his own servants' quarters. This man would come to ask questions of the young missionary and, when he was satisfied, returned to read some more. Underwood expressed confidence that "just as soon as the way is opened or in fact before it is publicly opened, as soon as I can speak the language well I shall be able to find all that I can attend to" (July 9, 1886).

In order to be ready for this, Heron asked the board to grant them "such additional sums as may be needed for opening up any work we can see our way clear to beginning" (February 1, 1886 in Letters of Pres. Church).

So 1886 ended on a mixed note. Much of encouragement had happened. Relationships with the court were good. Yet within the Presbyterian ranks there was dissension still needing resolution. If 1885 closed with uncertainty about the future of mission expansion, 1886 clearly ended that apprehension. The mission presence was well established, recognized, and encouraged. There were sufficient evidences of interest and response to the missionary's message to encourage the most melancholic of them all.

Growth and Development (1887)

Some indication of the success of the missionaries in the early months is reflected in a summary report Foulk sent to the secretary of state. In spite of the problems, he wrote, "the work of these missionaries cannot, to my mind, be too highly commended." He named each one and mentioned the work he was doing. Foulk informed the secretary of state that he had cautioned the missionaries against "indiscreet impulsiveness in propagating doctrines," and they had all expressed willingness to avoid troublesome areas. Apparently Foulk felt they had been successful. "With much tact and practical reason they have labored so as to secure the respect and kindly regard of the whole Corean people."

Foulk's conclusion sounded more like a mission report than a diplomatic dispatch:

> The spectacle presented by this little group of highly esteemed Americans, with their good work and bright homes in the midst of this dense, far-off people, so recently born into the knowledge of the outer world of nations, is pleasing in the extreme, is creditable to the people of America, and alike creditable to Corea, as well as a token of the most practical form that Corea is susceptible to progress and improvement, and worthy of the assistance she may receive and needs from the western nations that have recognized her as sister [U.S. Foreign Relations Papers 1886: 222-23].

To all of this Secretary Bayard replied, "I have received with pleasure and read with keen interest Mr. G. C. Foulk's dispatch relative to the colony of American missionaries in Seoul, and the successful prosecution of their good works" (July 31, 1886).

In January 1887 the queen, conversing with Annie Ellers, expressed a desire to see the American women ice skate. She invited Annie to bring her friends and use the pond in the palace compound. Naturally Annie's "friends" were her fellow missionaries. Their Majesties watched the skaters from the pavilion and when it started to snow, invited them all in for dinner (Ellers January 23, 1887 in Letters of Pres. Church).

This affair foreshadowed many significant and encouraging events which were to follow in 1887. In many ways this was a pivotal year in the first half decade of Protestant foundation-laying in Korea. Until that year the missionaries were so restricted and thus so cautious they were afraid to expand their work lest they attract unwanted attention and possible hostility.

As 1887 began, Henry Appenzeller reported three times the number of students (thirty) originally estimated for the new year. Of even greater significance, he received a name for his school on February 21 from the king himself. This was an overt and official expression of the approval of the king and his court regarding the presence of Appenzeller and his missionary colleagues.

As early as fall 1886 the president of the Foreign Office had made extensive inquiries about the school. He remarked that it should be given a name. When this was reported to Appenzeller, he invited the president to visit the school and give it an appropriate name. The king then sent a personal representative to pursue the matter further (January 15, 1887; February 21, 1887).

When these officials arrived, Mrs. Scranton, mother of the doctor and first missionary of the Women's Missionary Society, entertained them with a stereopticon show, a performance by some of the girls then studying with her, and "something to cheer the inner man." After this pleasant event, the officials reported back to the king. Soon the secretary of the Foreign Office came with names for Henry Appenzeller's school for boys and Mrs. Scranton's school for girls.

Appenzeller's school was named PaeJae Hakdang, "Hall for Rearing Useful Men." The name was written in Chinese characters, neatly framed on a board five feet by two feet painted in royal colors of bright red, blue, and gold. Both the royal colors and the style of calligraphy identified these name boards as having come from the palace and symbolized the king's acknowledgment and approval to all who saw them.

The significance of this naming and the hand-brushed signboard relate to Confucian traditions. For Koreans there was no mistaking. This school was officially recognized by His Majesty, King Kojong, and it gave the students a strong sense of pride to be attending PaeJae. It was suddenly *the* school, the center of progress and, not incidentally for Appenzeller, the foundation stone on which he would build the Methodist Church in Korea.

Appenzeller understood well the significance of the name and the king's calligraphy.

This name written in large Chinese characters has been properly framed and now hangs over the large front gate; the silent guardian of our educational work. It is the proclamation to all whom it may concern that the school has royal endorsement and encouragement. It is our charter [1887].

Similarly honored, Mrs. Scranton's school for girls was named "The Pear Blossom School," and Dr. Scranton's hospital designated "The Universal Relief Hospital." The government attached a guard to each of the missionaries, which was symbolic of its protection and approval.

All of this had a positive effect on public opinion regarding the Westerners. Already in March a report indicated an increase from thirty to forty-three students in PaeJae. One of them was meeting regularly with Appenzeller to study Christianity. Feeling more secure in his position, Appenzeller began for the first time to distribute copies of the Methodist Catechism, which Maclay had prepared earlier in Japan for the missionaries' use in Korea (March 13, 1887).

On April 13 Appenzeller and a Mr. Hunt of the customs service started on an overland trip to Pyongyang, no doubt the first such trip ever taken by foreigners in Korea (April 13, 1887). The two men rode the 185 miles on horseback and were accompanied by eight other horses loaded with the necessities of travel.

The list of items Appenzeller took is interesting and amusing: beds, blankets, sheets, rubber coats, extra shoes, old suit to ride in, extra one, needle, thread, pins, buttons, extra pair of suspenders, Japanese umbrella, full toilet set, white shirts, collars, night shirt, handkerchiefs, traveling cap, a pair of rubbers, jam, butter, milk, tea, alcohol stove, kettle to boil tea, sugar, potted meats, dried beef, cakes, knives, forks, spoons, skillet, stew pan, salt, box of flour, vinegar, pepper, a collapsible cup, and insect powder. Appenzeller kept a detailed diary of what he saw along the way. He was not only seeing the land but planning for mission stations which would some day be established in places other than Seoul.

On his return Appenzeller found word that his request for funds for a new school building was approved. In September, when Bishop Warren of the Methodist Church visited Korea, the school building was dedicated. It was seventy-six feet by fifty-two feet, one story high, built in a Renaissance style of architecture, and the first of its kind in Korea. It contained a chapel, four lecture rooms, a library, the principal's office, and a basement under half the building to be devoted to the industrial department. Though the building was incomplete, the large gathering of Korean dignitaries assembled for the public service of dedication made the event a memorable one. Henry wrote, "This is the first public service of a religious kind ever held by anyone in Korea" (September 14, 1887).

Two additional major advances were made in the work that year. On

Sunday, July 24, Appenzeller baptized his first Korean convert. He was Pak Choong Sang, a student in PaeJae school. Pak first learned about Christianity in Japan and was associated with Hayakawa, an attaché at the Japanese Legation whom Appenzeller had baptized on Easter. Understandably joyous, Henry wrote in his journal, "This is the beginning of our work here" (July 24, 1887). The year ended with sixty-three students enrolled in PaeJae and an average attendance of forty.

Thus in one year official recognition was secured for the educational and medical institutions of the Methodist mission, their first Korean convert was won, a preaching place was established and Appenzeller completed his new educational building.

The year's statistical report gives some indication of Methodist beginnings:

> Foreign missionaries—4; Assistants—3 [interesting that wives were referred to as assistant missionaries]; WFMS—2; native teachers—4; foreign teachers—3; probationers—4; adherents—150; conversions during the year—4; adults baptized—4; helpers—2; high schools—1; teachers in same—2; pupils—62; Sabbath schools—2; Sabbath scholars—20; parsonages or homes (missionary)—4; estimated value—$10,000; halls and other places of worship—1; value of schools and hospitals—$12,000 [October 9, 1887].

Missionary work for Henry Appenzeller was to preach the gospel, see people converted, and establish the church. Of the three, by far the greatest was preaching. Appenzeller loved to preach. From student days at Drew it was his greatest passion.

Yet preaching was never to be his full-time job. Instead he served as treasurer of the mission and later as superintendent. He supervised laborers in repairs and construction. He became involved in translation work, poring over French-Korean dictionaries to make Scripture portions available. He was an editor and spent hours organizing, collecting, and writing materials about Korea for publication both in Korea and abroad. He was instrumental in the founding of united mission projects, such as the Literature Society, the Bible Society, the Board of Translation, Seoul Union Church, Seoul Union Club, and the Seoul Foreign Cemetery.

But the work for which he was best remembered was PaeJae Boys' High School. It was both his greatest achievement and his greatest burden. To limit himself to the classroom and the principal's office when he preferred the provinces and the pulpits was a constant source of conflict. Though it was for him a second-choice ministry, Appenzeller strove so hard for the school as an evangelistic agency that his co-worker, Scranton, ranted, "I have heard nothing but school, school, school since I first entered upon missionary work" (September 3, 1889).

Scranton's quarrel with the school was not in relation to the "evangelize-civilize" issue but whether the school was a better "means" than the hospital for evangelizing. He said:

> I endorse with my whole heart the school plans and do not wish to see them less important . . . but I do not believe the school work is the best means now in Korea to reach people, nor that by which we can accomplish our ends most speedily.

In his preference for medicine as the best means, he concluded, "My point then is that the only ground on which we can best meet them at present is medicine. They want it, we have it to give and we should enter by the widest door" (September 3, 1889).

At the same time Appenzeller was willing to involve himself in education only by convincing himself and the board that it was in fact an evangelistic agency. He wrote his friend Wadsworth, "I have the great honor of founding the first Christian school, Protestant, of course, in Korea. I want it to be above everything else deeply spiritual. I want the students who come here to get converted" (February 14, 1887). He was convinced that "Christianity cannot be excluded when Western Civilization is taught" (*The Gospel in All Lands* 1887:409).

Not long after PaeJae was opened, Appenzeller began urging the board to send help to free him for more preaching. He was anxious to do evangelistic work and felt strongly that, for him, teaching was a poor second to preaching (July 1, 1886).

However much Henry Appenzeller wished to be free of PaeJae he never succeeded. As it grew, though, he became more aggressive in making it overtly Christian. In his mind PaeJae stood for evangelical Christianity, liberal Christian education, and the raising up of a "native ministry" for Korea. He felt nothing else justified the school's existence (June 11, 1901).

Though PaeJae was flourishing, other barriers faced Henry Appenzeller from the beginning. First was the language. Preaching was Appenzeller's first desire but he was to wait more than two years before he would be able to preach. This was his greatest trial. The Sunday sermon was such a regular habit for Methodist Appenzeller that it symbolized more than anything else his language limitations (June 1885; December 8, 1885; July 1, 1886).

Thus the climax of 1887 for Henry Appenzeller came on Christmas Day when he preached his first sermon in Korean. For that missionary the emotion of the moment must have been tremendous. He gave great care to the content, finally decided a positive approach was best. "Preach positive truth," he wrote. "Heathenism already has a super-abundance of negations" (undated Appenzeller sermon).

Appenzeller elaborated on his desire to avoid a negative approach. "We might have preached against wars, against official corruption, against con-

cubinage, against ignorance and laziness. We did nothing of the kind."
Quoting Paul, he said, "But we preached Christ" (1886).

The text was, "Thou shalt call his name Jesus, for he shall save his people
from their sins" (Matthew 1:21). Though his Korean was "with stuttering and
stammering tongue," it marked the beginning of his preaching ministry in
Korea. If the court knew of his public advocacy of Christianity, it apparently
chose not to make an issue of it. In a little more than two years Henry
Appenzeller had made significant accomplishments in the necessary and the
mundane.

For the Presbyterians, 1887 began with difficult interpersonal relations.
Burdened by the divisive wrangles and problems in his mission, Horace
Underwood proposed that the Presbyterians begin 1887 by getting together
to air grievances and try to resolve the difficulties. Allen reported, "Underwood's proposal was acted on and things are better." But still Allen wanted
permission to leave Korea. The problem did not cripple the work, however,
and gains were made in this crucial year (January 3, 1887; January 17, 1887).

The orphanage was full and turning down applications. Underwood was
already projecting beyond this orphanage to a school. Aware that in the
beginning the school could not be overtly Christian, he still felt that a start
was important. His orphanage only cared for young boys and the school
would be for older ones (January 22, 1887).

Thinking along similar lines Heron wrote, "It is only a question of a short
time before we can openly teach." He spoke of an increasing number of
requests for books and said, "The people seem so desirous of learning about
Jesus Christ" that he was frustrated at being "hampered by having to speak in
another tongue" (January 25, 1887 in Letters of Pres. Church).

The missionaries all recognized that their progress was astounding compared to Protestant beginnings in other parts of Asia. Underwood wrote that
his original expectation was to study language and translate Scriptures for the
first years. In contrast to his expectations, he noted, "Now we have been here
but a little over two years and the work has opened up so wonderfully that
there is really more to be done than we can undertake." His orphanage boys
were passing the Korean examinations well enough to receive official praise
(June 17, 1887).

A continuing conversation about methods of approach was going on
among Allen, Underwood, and Ellinwood. A new subject to further the
controversy was introduced by a number of baptisms in 1887. Underwood
reported by the middle of January that he planned to baptize twenty to thirty
converts of John Ross, China missionary, on the last Sunday of January. Ross
had become acquainted with Koreans while working near the border between Manchuria and Korea. The new Christians encouraged each other in
worship and fellowship and now arrived in Seoul seeking baptism from
Underwood.

Underwood examined them and found them "well aware of the fundamental and saving doctrines of Christianity." He warned them of the dangers involved in their taking such a step. He reported that they answered that "if God has saved them, though their king kill them, it will be all right." Another reportedly said, "Though my king cut off my head for obeying God, I will be all right."

The proscription against Christianity was still the law of the land, giving rise to these declarations, but there had not been any government action against those professing the Christian faith since the coming of the missionaries.

Heron also wrote about these baptismal candidates. He was surprised "at the readiness of their replies and the knowledge of the plan of salvation they showed and their earnestness in following out the teachings of the Bible" (January 22, 1887; January 25, 1887 in Letters of Pres. Church).

Allen was unhappy with Underwood about the baptisms. He felt mission work was still prohibited and thus Underwood had ignored Korean law. Underwood, drawing a fine line, countered that baptizing was not mission work but only the result of someone else's labors. In explanation he said,

Mission work proper is done every time that we speak to a Korean about Christ; every time that we welcome a seeker after truth; every time that we give a copy of the scriptures; and whenever we translate a verse of God's word into the Korean tongue [January 27, 1887].

Allen replied that missionaries were restricted from active mission work until the government lifted its prohibition. Underwood disagreed with Allen on the basis of the history of Protestant missions in other Asian countries. Citing China and Japan as examples he said, "I believe that the plan in all ages has been to work quietly wherever the way opened and then when the governments have learned of the good of Christianity they withdrew their restrictions." Furthermore, Underwood protested, he had scrupulously avoided proselytizing in the officially recognized institutions—hospitals, medical schools, and orphanages. But when these men sought him out and of their own accord, in spite of risk involved, requested him to baptize them, Underwood felt that "I as a minister of the gospel, as a missionary of the cross with my commission in my hand, and as a simple follower of Christ dare not deny it them." Thus he concluded, "I can find no warrant for such action denying them baptism either in the history of missions, in the story of the Acts of the Apostles or in the teaching of Christ" (January 27, 1887).

Heron wrote to Ellinwood asking, "Do you not feel like shouting over those baptisms?" Rather, Ellinwood cautioned Underwood, "As to the baptisms of which you speak, we should have been a little inclined to tremble. Better to bear on the side of safety than to run the risk of an explosion" (February 13, 1887; May 4, 1887 in Letters of Pres. Church).

The End of the Beginnings (1888–1890)

The success of the missionaries, the warm praise of the diplomats, and the gracious welcome of the king should not cloud the fact that these opening years were not free from problems. Koreans could not readily forget the hatred of foreigners stimulated by royal proclamation and personal experience.

It was a bit different in Korean officialdom. Many of these men had contact with the Western world and ways. Numbers of Korean officials visited America and attended diplomatic and court receptions for various occasions. They also shared many types of social events. Thus some of the false impressions were dispelled for them. They could not, however, ignore public opinion and fear.

Relations between Koreans and Americans were not confined to treaties, edicts, and proclamations. On one occasion a palace messenger came to Horace Allen requesting some of the hair oil the doctor was known to use. Allen's supply was depleted, but wishing to grant the royal request, he hurriedly mixed mint flavor with common sweet oil and sent it to the king. Similarly, Min Yong Ik, the royal nephew whose life Allen had saved, saw the American doctor's rubber boots and asked if he might have them. Allen polished them carefully and sent them over to the palace. But finding them too big, Min returned the boots to the doctor (February 10, 1885).

Such things are indicative of a level of awareness that went beyond mere formalities. Unfortunately, however, the background of hostility and suspicion mixed with superstition and ignorance led to many false rumors among the masses.

When the missionaries were seen using canned cream, Koreans had no idea where such milk came from. Unaccustomed to milking cows, they assumed it came from women's breasts. Thus the rumor began that missionaries were hiring men to use a strange gas to waken women from their sleep. The gas supposedly caused them to run from their rooms and when they did so they were caught and their breasts cut off to get the milk the missionaries used (Hulbert 1962:245).

Equally ridiculous but serious was the rumor apparently started when a Korean saw a missionary wife washing a pink piece of pork. Unaccustomed to eating pork and thus not recognizing the meat, the Korean hysterically assumed the missionaries had killed some of the babies kept at the hospital and were eating the flesh. It took an edict of the king to dispel this rumor but not before several Koreans were killed by a mob. Although they were innocently carrying their own children, they were suspected of being "baby runners" for the foreigners (Hulbert 1962:245).

Even such false rumors had their positive aspects for the missionaries' cause. The king issued a proclamation ordering parents to report missing children to the proper authorities and to cease the false reports against foreigners. Appenzeller felt "the government [has] shown commendable zeal in stopping the rumors and more, has shown itself friendly to foreigners" (June 22, 1888).

King Kojong's position was tenuous; on one hand he was active in squelching false rumors against foreigners while, on the other, proscribing the preaching of their Christian doctrines. He accepted their medical and educational work but still required missionaries who traveled outside of Seoul to sign a promise not to teach, preach, proselytize, or baptize.

Tolerance exceeded hostility nevertheless. As official recognition was attained, the mass recognition also began to come. Not only were false rumors dispelled but new evidences of good were becoming widely known. Missionaries were known, respected, imitated. In turn, the missionaries found Korea a more comfortable place to pursue the work of the heavenly kingdom they represented.

Mission work in the remainder of the decade from 1888 to 1890 continued to show a slow but steady progress. There were no major setbacks and if progress was slow, it was the general situation in Korea rather than anything specifically relating to the missionaries that accounted for it.

The new school building at Pae Jae was completed in 1888. The industrial department and a printing press were added to the institution. In the self-help program whereby students receive scholarships in exchange for work, students were involved with the printing press as well as more menial janitorial duties. Appenzeller was proud of this work program. "The readiness with which our boys do the work we assign them," he wrote, "is an encouraging feature of the work" (Methodist Annual Report 1888:338).

Dr. Scranton began a small medical school during this year. The annual report stated, "They are men who work for him in his dispensary and are taught the theory and practice together" (Methodist Annual Report 1888:339).

Scranton reported:

Our patients, as well as our students, come to us from all parts of the realm. The patients many times come with more faith in a cure than our diplomas will warrant us in promising or attempting. We have thus far been permitted to influence hundreds of Koreans toward a belief and reliance in what foreigners can do and teach, and we have relieved much suffering [*The Gospel in All Lands* 1888:373].

What was even more satisfying to Appenzeller was to be able to report:

Dr. Scranton . . . has begun evangelistic work in the hospital. Services are held there on Sundays. The in-patients are brought to the regular service. A literal bringing of the sick, lame, and blind, and religious books are for sale as well as medicines. We do not give away any religious books. *The hospital has now become a direct evangelical agency* [March 31, 1890; emphasis Appenzeller's].

Methodist statistics for the year show 11 members, 27 probationers, 165 adherents, 34 conversions, 34 baptisms, with 2 churches or chapels serving the needs of the people. Though still not free to preach openly, the Methodists were enjoying growth in their work (Methodist Annual Report 1888:339).

The main restraint on growth that the Presbyterians felt in 1888 was not prohibition in Korea but limitations of personnel and finance from the board. In the same year the Methodists received more than $28,000, the Presbyterians received only $14,000. For months Allen, Underwood, and Heron pressed the need for more personnel. Lamenting the board's lack of response, Underwood wrote in despair, "I have given up hope. I have written letter after letter. They seem almost to have forgotten they have a mission out here at all" (February 8, 1888).

During this time of stress from lack of adequate funds and personnel, Underwood became aware of a plan of missionary activity being suggested by John L. Nevius, missionary to China. Though the "Nevius Plan" encouraged self-support, self-government, and self-propagation, it also stressed a systematic Bible study program. Structured on three levels—local church, district (usually provincial), and national—it was a Bible training method effectively used in the Korean Protestant church (Clark 1961; Shearer 1966).

Underwood began conducting training sessions for Korean Christian leaders from various areas of the peninsula. The first of these was held in August 1888. The sessions were held in Seoul for a month at a time and emphasized basic doctrines of Christianity. In December Underwood started a theological class. In a chapel service "eleven young men stood up and before the whole assembly professed their faith and their determination, God helping them, to follow Him." He took them and other workers through "a short system of theology, teaching them singing and how to conduct meetings." In short he said he was teaching them how "to talk, read, and pray" (December 23, 1888).

In January 1889 Underwood noted that one year earlier there had been only twenty baptized converts. By 1889 there were over a hundred Presbyterian converts alone (January 7, 1889).

In the same month Henry Appenzeller reported a period of relative calm politically. Finally he was preaching regularly each Sunday, running a Sunday school, and holding a weekly prayer meeting. At PaeJae each day began with chapel, and a number of students were voluntarily studying the Bible. Some requested baptism. "The school is pervaded," he said, "with the Christian spirit and it is known as a missionary school."

In celebration of the New Year, the women of the Methodist mission entertained some of the highest government officials in the Appenzeller home. Appenzeller drew two significant conclusions from this event: "We are known as missionaries, and the Koreans are not afraid to call on us."

The year ended with little change statistically. The situation was summed up: "While we are not making great advance at present, we are holding our own and our missionaries are making the best possible use of such opportunities as they have" (Appenzeller January 28, 1889).

The Methodist quarterly report from Korea dated March 31, 1890, gave evidence of a more settled work. Appenzeller reported one church formally organized and thus able to come under the Methodist discipline. Attendance at the Sunday preaching service was from twenty-five to thirty. "For the first time in my experience," he wrote, "have I felt a pleasure and a comfort in preaching to the Koreans. I am encouraged at the outlook. We have strangers every Sunday."

Of PaeJae he said, "I think it is recognized among the Koreans that when a man attends our school he is either a Christian or a Christian sympathizer" (March 31, 1890). The compound was legally owned. Protestant Christianity was in Korea to stay.

Five years after the introduction of missionary activity the reactions of the Koreans were expressed in the words of one official to Henry Appenzeller: "We all know you are doing Christian work and that is what you are here for. We each know this personally but don't bring it up to us officially" (Methodist Annual Report 1887:315). It was this benign tolerance that permitted the steady growth.

King Kojong was always openly positive in his encouragement of the Protestant pioneers. He made sure that on national holidays or royal birthdays the missionaries were received in audience together with the advisers and with several departments of the government, the customs officials, and teachers of the regular government schools (January 21, 1901).

On January 1, 1890, the Methodists included four couples, two women, and one single man, all located in Seoul. The Presbyterians consisted of two families, two single women, and two single men in Seoul, with the Allens newly returned and established in Inchon. Three other groups arrived in late 1889: the Presbyterian Church of Victoria, Australia; Toronto University (Canada) YMCA; and an independent Canadian missionary who organized the Corean Itinerant Mission. All were in Seoul except the YMCA, which was located in Pusan.

The Methodists listed a total of 20 Korean workers of one kind or another, 9 members, 36 probationers, 165 adherents, average attendance on Sundays of 55, 29 conversions and 27 baptisms, 7 theological students, 81 high school students, 43 Sunday school students, and 2 churches. Thus only five years after the introductions there was a Methodist constituency of nearly five-hundred. The Presbyterians listed a total membership of one-hundred but, including staff and workers, Presbyterians were roughly equal to the Methodists.

The two missions were approximately equal in number of missionaries. Each was running a hospital. The Methodists maintained a school for boys and one for girls; the Presbyterians had an orphanage for boys and a school for girls. Methodists received more money but Presbyterians probably possessed more government connections.

But in 1890 each, Methodist and Presbyterian, could claim success. Success was not measured solely by numbers of converts, though compared to Protestant beginnings in China and Japan, the Korean pioneers were far ahead. They were settled, their presence acknowledged and even honored. Medical and educational institutions treated and taught hundreds of patients and students. Beyond this there were scores who accepted the faith proclaimed by the Protestants and were learning its tenets.

Korean Readiness and Acceptance

It is appropriate at this point to attempt to assess why Korea was ready to permit the presence of the Protestant pioneers, especially in the capital city so near the palace of the king. It may seem tautological to assert that if Korea was not "ready" to accept Protestant missionaries they would not have gained entry. Requests by the Protestant pioneers for permission to enter Korea clearly indicated their propagative motivation. Permission was not the result of misrepresentation or misunderstanding.

That the king permitted the missionaries to live in Seoul is also evident in a variety of ways. The king granted permission to enter, to buy property, to build buildings and establish medical and educational activities separate from or in place of previous government institutions. Furthermore, the king used the powers at his disposal to give rank to the missionaries and status to their institutions. Both of these expressions of official approval established the pioneers in the eyes of the Korean populace. Acceptance after years of relationships might be expected; that it came within the first weeks the missionaries were living in Seoul is remarkable.

Attempts to explain why Korea was ready to accept Protestant Christianity lack the most important source. There is no evidence in the court records or king's diaries of any Korean reflection on the coming of the missionaries. At least initially, factors in the East Asian world to which Korea had been tightly bound for centuries began to free it for relationships outside that world. The treaty with Japan in 1876 declared Korea independent. In the 1880s, at the urging of both China and Japan, Korea sought to establish relations with America. That China was in part seeking to strengthen its buffer-zone security against Japan while Japan desired similar protection against China does not change the impetus toward Korean-American relations. China and Japan agreed that the coming of America on the East Asian scene would also serve to balance the pressure of Russia and Britain in their attempts to gain a place in Korea.

More important, however, in explaining Korea's readiness to accept Protestant Christianity are factors in the immediate Korean context. The political turmoil on the domestic scene in Korea was troublesome. The forces for the traditional status quo arrayed against those for progress, each urging the king in opposite directions, made for a time of instability and confusion. That "tradition" and "progress" were merely banners under which factions and families fought for power only compounded the problem. Add to that the difficulty of either remaining secluded, which Korea did longer than any other Asian nation, or "opening" to the West, and the precarious position of the monarch becomes apparent.

The difficult nature of the Korean domestic political scene may have contributed to positive attitudes toward the coming of American missionaries. Favorable relations between American diplomats and the Korean court created a positive attitude toward Americans in general. With dissension and factionalism at home and uncertainty in the world of international relations, the Korean king was encouraged all the more to seek America's help.

If America was indeed disinterested but able to help, then the king welcomed relations. First diplomats, then missionaries represented a benevolent power wanting to be Korea's friend. The favorable image of America enhanced the image of the Protestant missionaries. Americans all—they worked closely with their diplomatic representatives.

Soon the king was requesting American advisers in his two most strategic areas of concern—foreign affairs and national defense. After a private audience at the king's request, Foote reported:

> In speaking of this subject, His Majesty remarked upon the friendly offers of assistance made by the United States; upon its having made the opening treaty of the Western Powers with Korea, and spoke at length of the great benefit Korea must derive from the assistance of competent Americans only at this time of her weakness amidst the threatening dissensions of the European powers. His Majesty closed his remarks by saying he would direct the Foreign Office to address a letter to the United States directly, with the hope of receiving an early and favorable reply [U.S. Foreign Relations Papers 1885:59].

Embarrassed by the lack of response from Washington, diplomats and eventually missionaries became stand-in advisers to the king in areas beyond their official capacities. The consequent building of positive relationships enhanced the missionary's presence in the court.

This acceptance of Protestant missionary presence may be said then initially to have been pragmatic national self-interest. The missionaries were

Americans and they were helpful in areas of great need for the king. With thousands of his people dying from smallpox and cholera and with others suffering from tumors and various injuries, medical relief was desperately needed. If this help was offered to the masses under the aegis of the king, all the more it would serve to ingratiate him with his subjects, to say nothing of caring for injuries and ills within his own palace.

Another unique situation in Korea as Protestant Christianity was introduced was the absence of any strongly entrenched religion. Almost every first-time visitor to Korea noticed the absence of religion. Henry Appenzeller wrote on his arrival:

These thousands of people within the walls of this city are practically without a religion. Ancestral worship is prescribed by law and therefore made obligatory. There is not a temple of any kind and Buddhist and Roman Catholic priests go about like thieves in the night. The former are not allowed in Seoul at all while the latter go about like mourners and are safe because a man in mourning must not be disturbed [August 1885].

A visitor in 1886 reported:

I was much interested and surprised at not seeing an idol or an idol-temple in the country anywhere, or in the city of Seoul. The people seem to have no love for idols, and they erect no temples to the gods. There is not a temple in the entire capital, and practically, the Koreans have no system of religion at all [*The Gospel in All Lands* 1886:2].

William Elliot Griffis noted in 1888, "The Koreans offer the spectacle of a nation without a religion and waiting for one. Hardly elsewise, humanly speaking, could the quick success of the American gospellers in Korea be explained. A church reared in four years" (*The Gospel in All Lands* 1888:371).

This apparent lack of religion was an interesting phenomenon. Of course there was Confucianism. But Confucianism had become more a rigid code for the legal and ceremonial conduct of government and the underlying support for Korean society. The missionaries may have been concerned about certain precepts of Confucian thought but they did not find a need to attack it immediately as a false religion totally incompatible with Christianity. Nor did Confucian civil servants and advisers to the king see any need to oppose the missionaries as long as they were willing to content themselves with the practice of medicine and the teaching of English.

Korea's two other background religions were even less a threat. Buddhism had been out of favor since the beginning of the Yi Dynasty in 1392. Its temples were remote, its priesthood weak. Shamanism was the most pervasive presence among the masses and the court. But Shamanism lacked any unifying institutional expression that would feel threatened by the coming of Protestant Christianity. It may have even represented a preparation for Christianity in making Koreans aware of a supernatural world (Shearer 1966: 26-31, 217-19).

Thus, while the encounter between Christianity and other religions has often been a central issue in the introduction of Christianity in other nations, in the Korea of 1885 it was almost no issue at all.

The difficulties surrounding the earlier introduction of Catholic Christianity created a greater problem to Protestant beginnings than the indigenous religions did. Because Catholic Christianity was perceived to be a political threat, thousands of Koreans had been killed for professing Catholicism. In the worst year of persecutions—1866—three French priests were also martyred. Following these martyrdoms a proclamation was issued against the "foreign learning" (Hulbert 1962:215). Anyone following it, teaching it, or in any way relating to it was to be put to death. And any foreigner in Korea was also to be put to death—considered to be a teacher of the hated religion.

It was this edict of 1866 that still proscribed the propagation of the gospel when Allen, Underwood, and Appenzeller arrived. Thus Allen as "Christian" and "missionary" would have raised old fears, suspicions, and hostilities. But Allen as American and doctor represented two areas of interest to the king. He wanted to get better acquainted with Americans and he needed the Western medicine. If in order to teach his own people the practice of medicine they needed to study English, then who better than Americans could teach it? Thus medicine and English broke down barriers and built bridges in this crucial period.

The king often inquired and was told of the difference between Catholic and Protestant Christianity (Allen May 9, 1886). However, the king's acceptance of the Protestants was certainly not based on a clear understanding of the historic differences between Catholics and Protestants. Rather, these Protestants seemed willing and anxious to work under the king's permission and to support and enhance his authority and image. Though he still did not openly permit them to preach, he did encourage them in every other way possible.

A third aspect in the initial acceptance of Protestant Christianity in Korea pertains to the attitudes and actions of the missionaries. Committed to a policy of caution and opportunism, they seized the opportunities available — seeking to establish confidence, and in time to expand to their larger and major concern, the preaching of the gospel. Furthermore, they were peaceable and supportive of the court's authority, unlike the earlier French Catholic introduction, which tended to antagonize or ignore the Korean ruling authority.

The Protestant missionaries began with the court. It may be questioned if this was a class-conscious attempt to ingratiate themselves with the ruling authority to the neglect of the masses. Rather, in a Confucian society, the missionary seeking to work with the masses and ignoring the court would have failed on two counts: the masses would have been afraid of involvement with hated foreigners whom the king threatened to kill, and the king would have considered such an act an insult to his own authority and position.

Thus when Horace Allen requested that his hospital be the king's hospital and that the king appoint the administration of it, he won both the favor of the king and the quick response of the masses. It was a strategic move and more than any other factor may account for the early success.

On a much less structured level of relationships, it may not be too facetious to suggest that the Americans were like real-life royal toys for the king and queen. In the normal order of relationships in the palace, everything functioned in rigid ceremony. The clothes, the greetings, the proper entrance and exit, the level of language—all was ritually and legally prescribed. With the Americans the king could be less formal. The images of the king and queen watching Annie Ellers and "her friends" ice skating; of the king proudly counting, "one, two, three" with enormous enjoyment are evidence of a more relaxed, tension-free relationship, which provided pleasure for the royal family.

These foreigners were a bright new presence in a possibly boring world of tradition and ritual. Treaties and trade agreements could be dealt with in proper government channels. Times of relaxation with these interesting creatures in his capital were subtly building mutual respect, admiration, and friendship. And the king was lavish with expressions of gratitude. In public proclamation, in name or conferred rank as well as in private parties, he spoke his continuing appreciation for these American missionaries (Allen February 4, 1885; June 1885; July 4, 1885; October 7, 1885; December 22, 1885).

As Christianity became more established an increasing number of Koreans were affected by the Protestant Christian presence in their land. One or two converts did not make much difference, but as the numbers grew the court found itself dealing with Christian subjects rather than foreign missionaries. These Christians did not threaten the power of the king, however. Rather, some of them served as interpreters at court, others were learning Western medicine, and in government examinations they proved as capable or more so than students of traditional Confucian schools.

Certainly no one factor explains conclusively the readiness of Korea to accept Protestant Christianity. But by an interesting convergence of factors the time was right and, in spite of some setbacks and concerns, Protestant Christianity succeeded in establishing a presence in the home of the "hostile hermit" and the "seashell."

6

Theological Assumptions of the Pioneers

Basic to the missionary's view of the world was its theological framework. The Protestant pioneers to Korea were shaped theologically by forces in their homes, their churches, and their schools, particularly college and seminary. This theological basis of the missionaries and their mission was reinforced by readings in mission periodicals like the Methodist's *The Gospel in All Lands* and the Presbyterian's *The Foreign Missionary.*

These magazines carried reports from various places where missionaries were working as well as articles by influential preachers and teachers in America who felt called to the task of stimulating interest in mission. Thus men like John F. Goucher, Rufus Anderson, and Arthur T. Pierson regularly wrote and spoke on the subject of missions. Goucher was a Methodist educator. Anderson was secretary of the American Board of Commissioners for Foreign Missions, and Pierson was a well-known Bible teacher. Numerous articles written by these men were published in mission magazines and provided support for mission based almost entirely on exposition of Scripture believed to be the divinely inspired and authoritative word of God to humankind.

Among the Korea pioneers, Henry Appenzeller left the most extensive record of attempts to explicate his missionary vision. Horace Allen's reports tended to be more matter-of-fact with little attempt at elucidating a scriptural mandate. Underwood, Heron, and Scranton matched neither Appenzeller nor Allen in the extent of their writing about mission in this early period. It may be assumed, however, that all shared a similar theological understanding of mission, though not all chose to articulate it at such length as Appenzeller did.

Theological Perspective

The Korea pioneers all grew up in pious Christian homes. Thus from very early their world and worldview were shaped by determinative theological assumptions. In these homes every possible influence was brought to bear on the life of the child, climaxing in the child's own personal appropriation of the work of Christ in behalf of his or her own soul. Quite often this "conversion" would take place at the close of special evangelistic services either in church, town hall, or campground. But for the future missionary, conversion was a necessary part of one's personal preparation for this life vocation. Preaching the funeral address for a missionary nurse who died in Korea, Appenzeller stressed this point.

> To be a successful missionary . . . a clear and distinct knowledge of sins forgiven is fundamental. Nothing can be substituted in its place. Physical vigor, intellectual ability, aptness to acquire a foreign language, the power of persistency, are all essentials to success. But unless one knows his sins are blotted out and that through grace divine he must become an heir and that he shall see the King in his beauty, he cannot hope to make a deep impression upon men who want and need forgiveness of personal sins [in Appenzeller Papers].

The Methodist board required its missionaries to have a conversion experience. One of the questions asked of applicants was, "Have you an experimental knowledge of salvation through the atonement of Jesus Christ our Lord?" Then it requested, "Answer this question somewhat in detail."

The Korea pioneers were all deeply influenced in the choice of their life's vocation by their days in college and seminary: Allen at Ohio Wesleyan, Underwood at New Brunswick, and Appenzeller at Franklin and Marshall and at Drew.

The prospectus for Franklin and Marshall College may be considered typical. President John Williamson Nevin in 1868 stressed not only a traditional liberal arts education but a religious life among the students and faculty centering around the college church. Students were expected to attend church each Sunday and to declare whether they had or not in answering a class roll call each week. In addition, chapel was held five times each week and attendance was compulsory (Dubbs 1903:328-29).

Emphasis on the personal piety of students and faculty was stressed even more at Drew. Methodists long opposed any type of theological education. Most old-line Methodists thought that choosing and preparing ministers was God's business and he needed no help from "mere mortal scholars." Those Methodists agitating for both educational and spiritual training were located mainly in the eastern United States and were referred to in negative terms as "New Thinkers." The controversy between emphasis on academic or spiritual matters colored the opening-day speeches in 1867 and continued down through the next century (Cunningham 1972:8).

Bishop Edmund S. Janes, a long-time advocate of theological training and a trustee of the seminary, speaking on opening day summed up the aims of Drew as well as those of the Methodists:

> We do not expect these who go from this institution simply to stand in the rank and file of Immanuel's army; nor to be mere gunners simply to load and fire, especially if they use a paper cannon. We expect every man to be competent to be a leader, and lead God's sacramental hosts

onward and upward until all the cohorts of error are driven from the world, and the standard of Christ is triumphant over all the lands [Cunningham 1972:64].

Referring to Drew as the West Point of Methodism, in a final burst of oratorical zeal he urged,

If a young man comes here with the lion in him, do not begin to pare his nails, or trim his mane, or tone his voice or tame his spirit, but let his claws grow, let his mane thicken, let his spirit wax until by his roaring he send terror to all the haunts of wickedness and dismay to all the dens of iniquity [Cunningham 1972:65].

In those days academic discipline was balanced by deep personal piety at Drew. Each day began and ended with prayers. There were prayers to open and close each class, prayers before and after every meal, even prayers "between dormitory and classroom." A highlight of every commencement at Drew was the Love Feast when graduates gave public testimony to their own personal religious experience (Cunningham 1972:83).

All this was to one purpose, to preach. There was great emphasis on the writing and delivery of sermons, but orderly presentation was not enough. The sermon was to be "delivered with such fire and feeling that a sermon would appear genuinely inspired . . . planned extemporization, in short" (Cunningham 1972:59).

It appears that the students accepted the situation without question. Drew was not just a place for the study of religion. It was a place where religious experiences were as important as religious studies. There was a "constant round of prayer, chapel meetings, invocations, testimonials, benedictions, and love feasts." The students came to Drew for just such reasons. "Drew's fundamental purpose, to fashion effective preachers of the gospel, pleased them. They wanted to be immersed in religion as well as academic theology" (Cunningham 1972:116).

Not all students were led into "full-time Christian service." But there was implicit in the atmosphere and often explicit in the founding principles of many Christian colleges that some type of full-time Christian work was the more noble pursuit.

Among the full-time professions, the missionary call was often viewed as the highest. Partly this related to the degree of personal sacrifice: anyone who would "give up" home, family, friends, and country to go to a "heathen country" to serve Christ was looked upon with a kind of holy awe usually reserved for saints.

Yet there was considerable ambivalence regarding missionaries. Some looked on them as misfits, as persons who through some martyr complex convinced themselves that they could render suitable service to God only by suffering, not only by the loss of all things (in the home scene) but through enduring hardship (in the country of service). By the same token, parents who dedicated their child to the Lord at birth were sometimes distressed when their child's dedication "led" him or her to leave home, family, and friends to serve in a far-off place.

Understanding of Mission

On a higher plane, the view of the missionary was a reflection of the church's view of mission. The world was the scope of the church's mission. Under orders from the Lord of the church they were to take the gospel "to every creature," "to all nations," "to the uttermost parts."

In a furlough address Appenzeller stressed the universal application and divine origin of the Christian message. Speaking of "the story of the cross," he said, "It is adapted for whatever race and in whatever region and whatsoever clime. We believe firmly and so teach that the gospel of Christ is the power of God unto salvation to everyone that believeth." Then Appenzeller asserted, "Missions are of divine origin" (1901).

Scriptural images pervaded the missionary's message. Appenzeller preached, "This story of Bethlehem's manger, of the agony in the garden, the atoning death on the cross, and the glorious and triumphant resurrection must be proclaimed" (1901).

He stressed the role of Christ by saying, "When God wishes to impress on the race a thought, He incarnates." Furthermore he suggested, "The history of the race teaches that all great movements, whether malevolent or benevolent, find their exponent in some individual." For examples of malevolent incarnations Appenzeller cited Jeroboam, Caiaphas, Julian, Voltaire, and Hume.

For Appenzeller on the positive side stood "Abraham, the friend of God; Moses, the lawgiver of Israel; David, the sweet singer of the chosen people; Paul, the great apostle to the Gentiles." Appenzeller concluded, "But rising above these as Teneriffe does above the sea is the man Christ Jesus who trod the winepress alone. It was He who wrought redemption for the race" (1901).

Henry Appenzeller made numerous references to Paul. Either he cited examples from the apostle's life or quoted scriptural injunctions from him. When the Methodist pioneer attempted to justify early meager results he quoted I Corinthians 1:26: "For ye see your calling, brethren, how that not many wise men after the flesh, not many mighty, not many noble, are called."

When Appenzeller wanted to explain his boldness in preaching he said, "For I am not ashamed of the gospel of Christ: for it is the power of God unto salvation to everyone that believeth; to the Jew first, and also to the Greek" (Romans 1:16). In telling of the content of his first sermon and explaining his positive approach, again a word from Paul gave support: "But we preach Christ crucified, unto the Jews a stumbling block, and unto the Greeks foolishness" (I Corinthians 1:23).

To describe the state of affairs in Seoul when he and his wife arrived, Appenzeller cited the experience of Paul as he came into Philippi (Acts 16:12-13), the chief city in that part of Macedonia, and found the women there ahead of him holding a prayer meeting by the riverside. "So when Mrs. Appenzeller and I came to Korea we found a missionary and his family in the chief city and they welcomed us as soon as they heard of our arrival in Chemulpo" (1901). Images drawn from Paul were frequent subjects of Appenzeller's sermons.

Not only for the larger framework on which the theory of missions was built, but in the ongoing activity there were appropriate analogies drawn from Scriptures, the mention of which would instantly communicate an idea and give it incontrovertible support. Appenzeller spoke of a Korean studying with him secretly.

> One of the students is studying the Word with me as is also a young official. They, like Nicodemus, come at night and sometimes they are unable to get away from their friends, but they seem to be interested and I hope the good Lord will speedily save them.

Appenzeller and his colleagues were never surprised by such evidences of interest on the part of Koreans. Nor did they lack confidence that the Koreans would respond. Appenzeller, writing of these secret students, said, "Others will follow for I am sure the work is of the Lord and He will prosper us" (April 1, 1887).

Often the scriptural image, the denominational concern, and the missionary's own call were intermingled. Appenzeller wrote:

> It is a privilege, as one Methodist to say as the great apostle, we are ready to preach to them that are in Rome also. That is, Methodism is ready in the opening of the twentieth century to preach the gospel anywhere and everywhere [1901].

Generally Scripture citations were used along two lines. On the one hand were stories symbolizing a principle; on the other were passages cited as literal injunctions or promises to be fulfilled. Examples of the former included the story of Jericho, of Joshua and Caleb, the Good Samaritan, and the parable of the fields.

Appenzeller found a framework on which to hang his story of Korea in the account of the spies in Joshua 13:26-33. First was the report of the land. At this point he described Korea. Second, the people who dwelled in the land, and third, their civilization was of interest in the biblical account, and so the missionary paralleled his accounts of Korea to this outline. There was no suggestion of actual comparison in the two stories but only that the scriptural setting provided the elements Appenzeller wished to stress in his report of

Korea. Presumably his hearers would be familiar with the Bible story and better remember Appenzeller's Korea report (1901).

Key Concepts: Rhetoric and Reality of Mission

In all the propagandizing for mission there were certain key concepts, which in one form or another continued to be expressed. In some cases a single word conveyed wide meaning to missionaries and their constituency. In some sense these words were determinative in the formation of the missionaries' image of themselves and their task. At the same time, when used by missionaries in the rhetoric of representation, the concepts served to perpetuate those images in the minds of the constituency and even the mission leadership.

Call

For the missionary, the most important word initially was "call." Closely related words were "led" and "faith." Behind this concept was the pattern of the men of scripture. Each one, according to the scriptural narrative, came to a point where he was confronted by God giving him a job to be done, usually at some cost but with promised blessing for obedience. Thus Abraham, Noah, Isaiah, Paul, and a host of others were "called" of God to go out by "faith" (Hebrews 11). They were "led" by God and in obedience they followed no matter what the cost.

To stress that mission was not a human idea but God's, Henry Appenzeller referred to Abraham. "Abraham did not call God and ask for the promised land. That is to say, the idea did not originate with Abraham but with God. So the idea of evangelism and conversion of the world is not from man but from God."

But Appenzeller also recognized the need for human agency. "This is God's work and ours. He will do His part, but we must do ours as well. We must go up and possess the land. We must do our part and in a profound sense, we must come up to help the Lord against the mighty" (1901).

Gospel

The missionary was "called" to "preach" and "teach" the "gospel." These words were taken from the words of Jesus and thus had the ring of authority to them. Appenzeller stressed:

The missionary goes to heathen lands for this one purpose. Your schools, your hospitals, your printing offices are all doing much good, . . . but let me tell you we go not to heathen lands to do people good in the common acceptance of the word. We go there to deliver our message that in Jesus Christ, by grace, God tasted death for every man. We go there to preach the gospel and we use everything, every agency, to help us in it [1901].

Heathen

A third word frequently used was "heathen." Preaching was to the heathen. Curiously, non-Christians in America were called "sinners" and non-Christians in other countries were called "heathen." Appenzeller also noted this phenomenon.

I suspect some of us at home think of the heathen as being a different being than ourselves. We see the pigtail of the Chinese, the peculiar shoes of the Japanese, and are attracted by the flowing robe of the Koreans and think them a very queer folk and congratulate ourselves that the Lord did not use the same dust in creating them as us.

Further, he continued, "American sinners are apt to think that other sinners have far more reason for gratitude for their salvation than they." He declared, "This doctrine is erroneous. These people are one with ourselves" (July 10, 1885).

Appenzeller, observing a market scene and the mass of people there, reported, "Our thoughts wandered to a time in the future when in that same market heathenism would be eradicated" (*The Gospel in All Lands* 1889: 527). He was confident of the ultimate victory of his mission. "Heathenism will die hard, but brother it *will die.*" He went on, "The church is in this conflict. Heathenism has shown herself powerless to satisfy the just desires of the human soul" (1901).

The Sense of Urgency

In all the enterprise there was a sense of urgency. Many of the images were militant and aggressive. Since many of them were taken from the apostle Paul—his pictures of soldiers (Ephesians 6: 10-17; II Timothy 2:1-7) and athletes (Hebrews 12:1; II Timothy 4: 7-8)—fighting and competing were frequently cited. It was the forces of righteousness against the forces of evil, the light against the dark, God against Satan.

As if planning strategy like a military commander, Appenzeller said:

Brethren, some of us crawled into heathenism, Romanism, and rebellion eight years ago. We got out but not where we crawled in. We are going back and now we want to take the center of the capital, the west, the east, the south, now closing in on the center. We don't expect to crawl back but to walk forward to victory [1901].

It has already been noted that both Allen and Appenzeller saw their mission as being to "take" Korea for Christ. Appenzeller wrote, "Brethren, as I understand our mission we are here to take this country for the Lord Jesus Christ . . . we will be satisfied with nothing less" (August 30, 1897).

Allen and Appenzeller's "take her" can only be understood in this militant metaphor. As missionaries they felt called to do battle against the "forces" of evil, darkness, superstition, and the heathen. They remained confident of ultimate victory.

The Heathen Are Lost

To portray the need and thus elicit a response was the concern underlying much missionary reporting. The picture was often graphic. One visitor to Korea reported, "Everywhere there is evidence of the greatest poverty. The houses of the people, the clothing, the food, are all of the poorest description. It would require the pen of Dickens to describe the dirt and squalor" (*The Gospel in All Lands* 1885:11).

Of the people, the same observer noted, "Indolence is written on every feature of their faces. Indeed it surprised me that people who were so lazy could be troubled to make so much noise, or could be roused to fight so easily" (*The Gospel in All Lands* 1885:11).

Appenzeller wrote:

From a human point of view, the moral condition of this people seems hopeless but I believe in the saving and elevating grace of God. Nothing less than the blood of Christ applied to their hearts can save them from their sins. They are waking up to a sense of their temporal condition. May at the same moment their eyes be opened to their spiritual need. Lord, hasten the day [undated].

Griffis felt America carried a special responsibility for Korea. "We Americans," he wrote,

must give the Gospel to Korea. Our diplomacy opened her doors, and tempted her into the world's market-place, introducing likewise modern debts, diseases, and disorders, social and political; and *we* should be first to heal and bless, with the blessing wherewith we ourselves have been blessed of God. Shall we do it? [*The Gospel in All Lands* 1888: 370-71].

Methodist Dr. Scranton, pleading for more workers for Korea, asked:

Did you ever miss a meal in your life? Did you ever know what it is to have days of hunger and heartache, too? Don't you . . . some hearing reader . . . know that the whole world is hungering and suffering, and that many are continuing in their troubles until you go to help them? And haven't you drunk so deeply yourself of the water of life that the taste of that pure satisfying draught makes you want to tell others and share it with them? Won't someone hear? [*The Gospel in All Lands* 1890:429].

Salvation through Christ

Appenzeller emphasized this theme in a sermon on "adoption" from I John 3:2.

"Without the shedding of blood there is no remission of sins." We are justified by faith and at the same time born again, and on this foundation and on this as a preparation we are received into the divine family. Our sonship is grounded in Calvary, at the cross, under the blood we first cry, Abba, Father. This necessarily does away with claptrap talk so frequently and thoughtlessly indulged in of the fatherhood of God and the brotherhood of man, because it overlooks or fails to recognize the foundation on which the relationship between God and man is made [March 16, 1902].

Before He Comes

Appenzeller and his colleagues expected ultimate eschatalogical victory for their mission. The obituary for Henry Appenzeller read, "In all his efforts he was moved by the highest optimism and had the greatest faith in the ultimate triumph of Christ's church in the world" (1902).

Appenzeller had said:

We go to heathen countries not so much to get 100 or 200 converted —glad for that—as to point them unto Jesus, great captain of our salvation. To tell them that the prince of this world is judged and cast out. Heathenism looks back and down for help. We look up and out. Lo, our leader from the skies waves and before us the glorious prize. The prize of victory [undated].

The Forum of the Propaganda

Just as in the missionary's role as image-maker, the forum for the propaganda included letters, reports, and articles addressed to mission executives, official mission publications, family, and friends. The intended audience affected the emphasis in the rhetoric.

The propagandizers were usually missionaries, but often mission executives were called upon to "promote" the cause of mission in local churches, preachers' meetings, annual conferences, colleges, and seminaries. Then there were the pastors-at-large like A. T. Pierson, who became much in demand to represent mission interests.

In all there was a mix between fresh reports "from the field" and a scriptural explication of the need for involvement. This latter was often called "the Bible basis of missions." The Scripture and the report supported and reinforced each other as an authoritative word from the Lord.

And so the cycle was complete. The pioneers themselves responded to the rhetoric of mission and specifically the new opportunity in Korea. They found trial and hardship, which they had expected. They found possibility and promise, which was greater and realized sooner than they had any reason to anticipate. If there were no mass conversions in these beginning years, there was an acceptance of them as missionaries, and appreciation for their work, and one by one there were those who came to follow the One in whose name the pioneers had come.

Bibliography

Korean Language Publications

CCIG, *see* Chungchee Illgee

Chang, ToBin.
   1935   *Hangook Malnyonsa* (History of the Last Years of Hangook).
            3 vols. Seoul: Tokyung Sulim

Chindan Hak Hwa Pyung.
   1970   *Hangook Sah* (Korean History). Seoul: Oolyu Moon Co.

Choi, NamSun.
   1946   *Kookmin Chosun Yuksah* (History of the Korean People).
            Seoul: Dong Mung Co.,

Choo, ChaeYong.
   1970   *Kaetollik Saheh Ongoui* (Catholic History). Seoul: Korean
            Catholic Central Publishing Co.

Chosun Sinsa Pogam (Mirror of Korean Gentleman). Seoul: Chosun
   1912   ChulpanHyophoe.

Chung, IngWha.
   1940   *Chosun Yehsookyo Changnohwaesah* (History of the Korean
            Presbyterian [Jesus] Church). Seoul: General Conference
            Office.

Chungchee Illgee, CCIG (Diary of Political Affairs).
   n.d.

Hangook Chongyo Chongnam (An Overview of Korean Religion).
   1973   Seoul: Sunghwasah.

Hangook Sah (History of Korea). Seoul: Chindanhak Co.
   1961

Illsung Nok, ISN (Daily Records concerning National Affairs).
   n.d.

ISN. *see preceding entry.*

KHWM, *see* Koo Hangook Waegyo Moonsuh.

Kim, ChoonPae.
   1966   *Hangook Kyoihwae Sungchangsah* (History of Korean
            Church Growth). Seoul: Taehan Kidokyo Soonan Sahwae.

1969   *Hangook Kidokyo Soonan Sahhwa* Seoul: Sungmoon Haksa.

Kim, KwangSoo.
1971   *Hangook Kyohawe eh Ohjae wah Oneul* (Korean Church Yesterday and Today). Seoul: Sejong Moonwhasa.

Kim, TeukHwang.
1971   *Hangook Chongyosa* (History of Korean Religion). Seoul: Eppel Choon Pansah.

1973   *Hangook Sasangsah* (History of Korean Thought). Seoul: History of Korean Thought Research Center.

Kim, YangSun.
1956   *Hangook Kidokyo Haebang* (Korean Christianity and the Korean War). Seoul: Yehsookyo Changnohkyo Kyobook Bo.

Kojong Sillak, KS (The Annals of King Kojong).
n.d.

Koo Hangook Waegyo Moonsuh, KHWM (Diplomatic Documents of Old
n.d.   Korea).

Kotae Minchok Moonhwa Yungoosa.
1970   *Hangook Moonhwasah Tae Kaeyuk Chongkyo Chulhaksa* (Outlines of Six Main Philosophies of Religion in Korean Culture). Seoul: Minjok Moonhwa Yungoosah.

KS. *see* Kojong Sillak.

Kwak, AhnJun.
1970   *Hangook Kyohwaesah* (History of the Korean Church). Seoul: Taehan Kitokyo Suhhwae.

Lee, ChunYung.
1970   *Sungyul Kyohwaesah* (History of the Korean Holiness Church). Seoul: Kotokyo Taehan Sungyul Kyohwae Choolpansa.

Lee, HoOon.
1970   *Hangook Kyohwae Chokisah* (History of the Early Korean Church). Seoul: Taehan Kitokyo Suh hwae.

Lee, KeePaek.
n.d.   *Hangook Sah Sillon* (Record of Korean History).

Lee, KwangLin.
n.d.   *Kae Hwasah Yungoo* (Research in the Beginnings of Korean History).

Lee, PyongDo.
1972   *Hangooksa Taegwan* (A One-Volume History of Korea). Seoul: Pomoongak.

Lee, Wonsoon.
  1971   *Hangook Chunjukyo Hwaesah* (History of the Catholic
              Church in Korea). Seoul: Pam Goodang.

MGTSSG, *see next entry.*

Migook Tongsang Silgee, MGTSSG (Record of American Commerce).
  n.d.

Min, KyongBae.
  1972   *Hangook Kitokyo Hwaesah* (History of Korean Christianity).
              Seoul: Taehan Kitokyo Suhhwae.

Pyon, ChongHo.
  1959   *Hangook Kitokyosa Kaeyah* (An Outline History of Korean
              Christianity). Seoul: Shim Oowon.

Seungjungwon Illgee, SJWIG (The Diary of the Royal Secretariat).
  n.d.

SJWIG, *see preceding entry.*

TMKG, see next entry.

Tongmoon Kwangee, TMKG (Record of the Bureau of Interpreters).
  n.d.

Waesah Illgee, WIG (Diary of Japanese Affairs).

Yang, JuSam.
  1926   *Chosun Nam Kamneehwae 30 Nyum Kinyumpo* (30-Year
              Memorial History of the Korean Southern Methodist
              Church). Seoul: Korean Southern Methodist Church.

Yi, NungHwa.
  1925   *Chosun Kitokyo Kup Waegyosa* (History of Christianity and
              Foreign Relations of Korea). Seoul: Chosun Kitokyo
              Changmunsa.

Yi, PyungDo.
  1949   *Hangook Kuksa Taegam* (An Outline History of Korea).
              Seoul: Tongjisa.

Yu, DongSik.
  1967   *Hangook Chongyo wa Kitokyo* (Christianity and Korean Reli-
              gions). Seoul: Korean Bible Society.

Yu, HongYul.
  1962   *Hangook Chunjukyo Hwaesa* (History of the Catholic
              Church in Korea). Seoul: Catholic Press.

English Language Publications

Allen, Horace N.
The Horace Allen Papers in the New York Public Library.

1901   A *Chronological Index*. Seoul: Private printing.

1901–2   *Supplement to a Chronological Index*. Seoul: Private printing.

1904   *Korea: Fact and Fantasy*. Soeul: Methodist Publishing House.

1908   *Things Korean*. New York: Fleming H. Revell.

Anderson, Rufus.
1845   *The Theory of Missions to the Heathen*. A sermon at the ordination of Mr. Edward Webb as a missionary to the heathen. Ware, Massachusetts, October 23, 1845. Boston: Press of Crocker and Brewster.

1869   *Foreign Missions: Their Relations and Claims*. New York: Charles Scribner and Co.

Annual Report of the Missionary Society of the Methodist Church.

1819–90

Appenzeller, Henry G.
The Henry G. Appenzeller Correspondence, The United Mission Library, New York.

The Henry G. Appenzeller Papers, New York: The Missionary Research Library, Union Theological Seminary.

1890   "The PaeJae Haktang of Korea." *The Gospel in All Lands,* XVI, 115.

Bailey, Thomas A.
1969   *A Diplomatic History of the American People*. 8th ed. New York: Meredith Corp.

Barr, Pat.
1970   *Foreign Devils*. Harmondsworth, England: Penguin Books.

Beaver, R. Pierce, ed.
1967   *To Advance the Gospel, Rufus Anderson*. Grand Rapids: W. B. Eerdmans.

Bemis, Samuel Flagg.
1955   *A Diplomatic History of the United States*. New York: Henry Holt and Co.

Beyerhaus, Peter and Lefever, Henry.
1964   *The Responsible Church and the Foreign Mission*. Grand Rapids: W. B. Eerdmans.

Bishop, Isabella Bird.
1970   *Korea and Her Neighbors.* Seoul: Yonsei University Press.

Blacker, Carmen.
1969   *The Japanese Enlightenment, a Study of the Writings of Fukuzawa Yukichi.* London: Cambridge Univ. Press.

Boorstin, Daniel J.
1973   *The Americans: The Democratic Experience.* New York: Random House.

Brauer, Jerald C., ed.
1968   *Essays in Divinity.* Vol. 5: *Reinterpretations in American Church History.* Chicago: Univ. of Chicago Press.

Cable, E. M.
1938   "U.S.-Korean Relations, 1866-1871." *Transactions of the Royal Asiatic Society—Korea Branch* 28: 1-202.

Cary, Otis.
1909   *A History of Christianity in Japan.* 2 vols. New York: Fleming H. Revell.

Christian Advocate (California).
1885   Report by George Adams, February 25, 1885.

Choe, Ching Young.
1972   *The Rule of the Taewongun, 1864–1873.* Cambridge: Harvard Univ. Press.

Chu, Tung-Tsu.
1962   *Local Government in China under the Ch'ing.* Cambridge: Harvard Univ. Press.

Chung, Chai-Sik.
            'Protestantism and the Formation of Modern Korea, 1884–1894'. Microfilm copy.

Clark, Allen D.
1961   *History of the Korean Church.* Seoul: Christian Literature Society (original ed. 1930).

1973   *Prayer Calendar of Christian Missions in Korea and General Directory.* Seoul: Christian Literature Society.

Conroy, Hilary.
1960   *The Japanese Seizure of Korea, 1868–1910.* Philadelphia: Univ. of Pennsylvania Press.

Cook, Harold F.
1972   *Korea's 1884 Incident.* Seoul: Royal Asiatic Society, Korea Branch.

Cunningham, John T.
1972   *University in the Forest.* Madison, N.J.: Afton Publishing Co.

Dallet, Ch.
1874   *Histoire de l'église de Corée.* 2 vols. Paris: Victor Palme.

de Bary, Wm. Theodore; Chan, Wing-Tsig; and Watson, Burton.
1960   *Sources of Chinese Tradition.* New York: Columbia Univ. Press.

Dennett, Tyler.
1963   *Americans in Eastern Asia.* New York: Barnes and Noble (original ed. 1922).

1923   "Early American Policy in Korea, 1883–1887." *Political Science Quarterly* 38, no. 1: 81-103.

Dubbs, Joseph Henry.
1903   *History of Franklin and Marshall College.* Lancaster, Pa.: Franklin and Marshall Alumni Association.

Fairbank, John K.
1958   *The United States and China.* Cambridge: Harvard Univ. Press.

1968   *The Chinese World Order.* Cambridge: Harvard Univ. Press.

1969   "Assignment for the Seventies." *The American Historical Review 74,* no. 3 (February).

1974   *The Missionary Enterprise in China and America.* Cambridge: Harvard Univ. Press.

Fairbank, John K.; Reischauer, Edwin O.; and Craig, Albert M.
1965a   *East Asia: The Modern Transformation.* Boston: Houghton Mifflin Co.
1960   *Ch'ing Administration Three Studies.* Cambridge: Harvard Univ. Press.

1965   *China's Response to the West.* New York: Atheneum.

First Annual Report of the Korean Government Hospital
1886

The Foreign Missionary
1880–86   Vols. 39–45.

Foulk, George C.
         The George C. Foulk Papers in the New York Public Library.

Fung, Yu-Lan.
1968   *A Short History of Chinese Philosophy.* New York: Free Press.

Gale, James Scarth.

1909a   *Korean Sketches.* New York: Young People's Mission Movement.

1909b   *Korea in Transition.* New York: Young People's Mission Movement.

1972   *History of the Korean People.* With a biography and annotated bibliography by Richard Rutt. Seoul: Taewon Publishing Co.

The Gospel in All Lands.

1885–96   Vols. 11–22.

Goucher, John F.

1881   *Young People and the World's Evangelization.* New York: Young People's Missionary Movement.

1882   "The Annual Missionary Sermon Preached before the Baltimore Annual Conference During its 98th Session."Baltimore: The Conference.

1903   *Young People and Missions.* Addresses delivered before the Eastern Missionary Convention of the Methodist Episcopal Church, Philadelphia, Pa., October 13-15.

1911   *Growth of the Missionary Concept.* The Nathan Graves Foundation Lectures delivered before Syracuse University. New York: Eaton and Maine, 1911.

Griffis, William Elliot.

The William Elliot Griffis Collection at Rutgers University Library.

1886   *The Mikado's Empire,* 5th ed. New York: Harper and Brothers.

1907   *Corea, the Hermit Nation.* New York: C. Scribner's Sons (first published in 1882).

1912   *A Modern Pioneer in Korea: Henry G. Appenzeller.* New York: Fleming H. Revell.

Han, Woo-keun.

1970   *The History of Korea.* Translated by Lee, KyungShik. Edited by Grafton K. Mintz. Seoul: EulYou Publishing Co.

Harrington, Fred Harvey.

1966   *God, Mammon, and the Japanese: Dr. Horace N. Allen and Korean-American Relations, 1884-1905.* Madison: Univ. of Wisconsin Press.

Henderson, Gregory and Yang, Key P.
1958   "An Outline History of Korean Confucianism," parts 1 and 2. *The Journal of Asian Studies* 18, pt. 1, no. 1 (November): 81-101; pt. 2, no. 2 (February 1959): 259-76.

Hudson, Winthrop S.
1961   *American Protestantism.* Chicago: Univ. of Chicago Press.

Hulbert, Homer B.
1962   *History of Korea.* 2 vols. New York: Hilary House Publishers (original ed. 1905).

Irlye, Akira.
1967   *Across the Pacific.* New York: Harcourt Brace and World.

Jones, George Heber.
1910   *The Korea Mission of the Methodist Episcopal Church.* New York: Methodist Board of Missions.

Kim, C. I. Eugene, and Kim, Han-Kyo.
1967   *Korea and the Politics of Imperialism, 1876–1910.* Berkeley: Univ. of California Press.

Kim, Chang-mun, and Chung, Jae Sun, ed.
1963   *Catholic Korea Yesterday and Today.* Seoul: Catholic Press.

Kitagawa, Joseph M.
1966   *Religion in Japanese History.* New York: Columbia Univ. Press.

Knox, George W.
1884   "The Condition of Korea." *The Foreign Missionary* XLIII, n. 4.

Korea in Brief.
1971   Korean government publication.

Korea, Its Land, People and Culture of All Ages.
1960   Seoul: Hakwonsa, Ltd.

Lach, Donald F.
1965   *Asia in the Making of Europe.* Vol. 1: *The Century of Discovery.* Bk. 1. Chicago: Univ. of Chicago Press.

Latourette, Kenneth Scott.
1929   *A History of Christian Missions in China.* New York: Macmillan Co.

1964   *A Short History of the Far East.* Toronto: Macmillan Co.

1970a   *A History of the Expansion of Christianity.* Vol. 3: *Three Centuries of Advance, 1500–1800.* Grand Rapids: Zondervan Publishing Co.

1970b   *A History of the Expansion of Christianity*. Vol. 6: *The Great Century, North Africa and Asia, 1800–1914*. Grand Rapids: Zondervan Publishing Co.

Lee, ChongSik.
1965   *The Politics of Korean Nationalism*. Berkeley: Univ. of California Press.

Letters of the Presbyterian Church in the United States of America.
1884–1911 Korea Missionaries Incoming and Outgoing. Philadelphia: The Presbyterian Historical Society, microfilm.

Lin, T. C.
1935   "Li Hung Chang: His Korea Policies, 1870–1885." *The Chinese Social and Political Science Review* 19 (1935–36): 202-33.

Liu, KwangChing.
1963   *Americans and Chinese: A Historical Essay and a Bibliography*. Cambridge: Harvard Univ. Press.

McCune, George M., and Harrison, John A., eds.
1951   *Korea-American Relations*. Vol. 1: *The Initial Period, 1883–1886*. Berkeley: Univ. of California Press.

MacGavran, Donald A.
1970   *Understanding Church Growth*. Grand Rapids: W. B. Eerdmans.

McKensie, F. A.
1969   *The Tragedy of Korea*. Seoul: Yonsei University Press.

Maclay, R. S.
1896a   "A Fortnight in Seoul, Korea, 1884." *The Gospel in All Lands* 22 (August): 354-56.

1896b   "Commencement of the Korea Methodist Episcopal Mission." *The Gospel in All Lands* 22 (August): 498-502.

Marty, Martin E.
1970   *Righteous Empire*. New York: Dial Press.

May, Ernest R., and Thomson, James C., Jr., eds.
1972   *American–East Asian Relations: A Survey*. Cambridge: Harvard Univ. Press.

Meskill, Johanna M.; Meskill, John; and Embree, Ainslie T.
1971   *The Non-European World, 1500–1850*. Glenview, Ill.: Scott Foresman and Co.

Moffett, Samuel Hugh.
1962   *The Christians of Korea*. New York: Friendship Press.

Neill, Stephen.
1964   *A History of Christian Missions.* Harmondsworth, England:
            Pelican Books.

Neill, Stephen; Anderson, Gerald H.; and Goodwin, John.
1970   *Concise Dictionary of the Christian World Mission.* London:
            Lutterworth Press.

Nelson, M. Frederick.
1946   *Korea and the Old Orders in Eastern Asia.* Baton Rouge:
            Louisiana State Univ. Press.

Nevius, John L.
1958   *Planting and Development of Missionary Churches.* Philadel-
            phia: Presbyterian and Reformed.

New York Times.
1880–90

Noble, Harold J.
1933   "The United States and Sino-Korea Relations, 1885–87."
            Pacific Historical Review 2: 191-304.

Oppert, Ernest.
1880   *A Forbidden Land.* London: Sampson Low, Marston, Searle,
            and Rivington.

Paik, George.
1971   *The History of Protestant Missions in Korea, 1832–1910.*
            Seoul: Yonsei University Press.

Palmer, Spencer J., ed.
1963   *Korean-American Relations: Documents Pertaining to the Far
            Eastern Diplomacy of the United States.* Vol. 2: *The Period of
            Growing Influence, 1887–1895.* Berkeley: Univ. of Califor-
            nia Press.

1967   *Korea and Christianity.* Seoul: Hollym Corp. Publishers.

Parkinson, C. Northcote.
1965   *East and West.* New York: Mentor Books.

Paullin, Charles Oscar.
1910   "The Opening of Korea by Commodore Shufeldt." *Political
            Science Quarterly* 25, no. 3: 470-99.

Pierson, Arthur T.
1886   *The Crisis of Missions.* New York: Robert Carter and Bros.

1891a   *The Divine Enterprise of Missions.* New York: Baker and
            Taylor Co.

1891b   *The Greatest Work in the World.* New York: Fleming H.
            Revell.

1894   *The New Acts of the Apostles.* New York: Baker and Taylor
            Co.

Reischauer, Edwin O.
1969   *The United States and Japan.* New York: Viking Press.

Reischauer, Edwin O., and Fairbank, John K.
1960   *East Asia, the Great Tradition.* Boston: Houghton Mifflin
            Co.

Rhodes, Harry A.
1934   *History of the Korea Mission, Presbyterian Church U.S.A.,
            1884–1934,* vol. 1. Seoul: Chosen Mission of the Presbyte-
            rian Church, U.S.A.

Ro, KwangHai.
n.d.   "Power Politics in Korea and Its Impact on Korean Foreign
            and Domestic Affairs, 1882–1907." University Microfilms;
            University of Michigan, Ann Arbor, Mich. Film No. 66-10,
            191.

Ross, John.
1879   *History of Corea.* Paisley: J. and R. Parlane.

Sansom, G. B.
1950   *The Western World and Japan.* New York: Alfred A. Knopf.

Sauer, C. A.
1934   *Within the Gate.* Seoul: Methodist News Service.

Scranton, William F.
            The William F. Scranton Correspondence at the United
            Mission Library, New York.

Shearer, Roy E.
1966   *Wildfire: Church Growth in Korea.* Grand Rapids: Wm. B.
            Eerdmans.

Shedd, Clarence P.
1934   *Two Centuries of Student Christian Movements.* New York:
            Association Press.

Sitterly, Charles Fremont.
1938   *The Building of Drew University.* New York: Methodist
            Book Concern.

Stokes, C. D.
1947   "History of Methodist Missions in Korea, 1885–1930." A
            Xerox copy of an unpublished dissertation, Yale Univer-
            sity.

Strong, Josiah.
1963   *Our Country.* Cambridge: Belknap Press of Harvard Univ.
            Press.

Treat, Payson J.
  1934   "China and Korea, 1885–1894." *Political Science Quarterly*
           44: 506-43.

  1970   *Japan and the United States, 1853–1921.* Stanford: Stanford
           Univ. Press.

Tsiang, T. F.
  1931   "Origins of the Tsungli Yamen." *The Chinese Social and
           Political Science Review* 15 (1931–32): 92-97.

  1933   "Sino-Japanese Diplomatic Relations, 1870–1894." *The
           Chinese Social and Political Science Review*, 17: 1-106.

Tsunoda, Ryusaku; de Bary, Wm. Theodore; and Keene, Donald, eds.
  1967   *Sources of Japanese Tradition*, vol. 2. New York: Columbia
           Univ. Press.

Underwood, Horace G.
           See Letters of the Presbyterian Church in the United States
           of America.
  1908   *The Call of Korea.* New York: Fleming H. Revell.

Underwood, Lillie H.
  1904   *Fifteen Years among the Top-Knots.* New York: American
           Tract Society.

  1918   *Underwoods of Korea.* New York: Fleming H. Revell.

U.S. Department of State.
  1866–90 *United States Foreign Relations.* Washington D.C.: Govern-
           ment Printing Office.

  1949   *United States Relations with China.* Washington D.C.: Divi-
           sion of Publications, Office of Public Affairs.

Vinton, C. C.
  1895   "Statistics of the Protestant Churches in Korea." A paper
           read before the Decennial Conference of Christian Mis-
           sions in Korea, October 10, 1895. *The Korean Repository* 2:
           382-85.

Warren, Max, ed.
  1971   *To Apply the Gospel. Selections from the Writings of Henry
           Venn.* Grand Rapids: Wm. B. Eerdmans.

Wasson, Alfred W.
  1934   *Church Growth in Korea.* New York: International Mission-
           ary Council.

Weems, Benjamin B.
  1964   *Reform, Rebellion, and the Heavenly Way.* Tucson: Univ. of
           Arizona Press.

Yang, C. K.

    1970   *Religion in Chinese Society*. Berkeley: Univ. of California Press.

You, InJong.

               "The Impact of the American Protestant Missions on Korean Education, 1885–1932." University Microfilms. University of Michigan, Ann Arbor, Mich. Film No. 68-2254.

Yukichi, Fukuzawa.

    1960   *The Autobiography of Fukuzawa Yukichi*. Translated by Eiichi Kiyooka. Tokyo: Hokuseido Press.

    1969   *An Encouragement of Learning*. Translated by David A. Dilworth and Umeyo Hirano. Tokyo: Sophia University.

Index

Allen, Horace Newton, 23
  arrival in Korea of, 1, 15-22, 62, 78, 82
  hospital of, 31, 33-38, 63-65, 83
  images of Korea of, 58, 59, 91
  at Korean court, 18-22, 33-37, 44, 63-65, 67, 75, 82, 83
  and Methodists, 31, 32, 34, 35, 42-44, 64
  and Presbyterians, 32, 36-38, 44, 64, 67, 73, 74
America
  advisers from, 9, 10, 21, 80
  envoy of, 2, 8, 29
  image of Korea of, 2-4, 46, 49, 53, 54, 56
  legation of, 8, 12, 14, 17, 18, 20, 21, 31, 32, 39, 40
  Navy department of, 47
  president of, 53, 54
  relations with Korea of, 2, 3, 7, 10, 13, 19, 30, 81
  Secretary of State of, 8, 46, 68
  State Department of, 49, 50
Anderson, Rufus, 84
Anglo-Japanese College, 14
Appenzeller, Henry G.
  application for Korea of, 11
  early preparation of, 23-28, 85
  en route to Korea, 22, 23, 28-32, 34, 35
  images of Korea of, 56-59, 81, 84
  and Korea beginnings, 38-45, 82
  language study of, 63
  teaching of, 62-64, 69-73, 76-78
  understanding of mission of, 87-92
  see also Methodists; Pae Jae Boys High School

Bayard, Thomas F. (secretary of state), 68
Buddhism, 81

Catholics, 41, 63
  persecution of, 15, 48, 82
  see also Christianity
Chefoo, 48, 49
Chemulpo, 7, 16, 29, 31, 32, 34, 37, 39, 40, 43, 53, 58
China
  attitudes to Korea of, 50
  compared to Korea, 53
  Confucian culture of, 5
  as Korea's neighbor, 2, 6-9, 15, 29-31, 39, 46
  mission activity in, 3, 6, 17, 20
  Peking, 8, 16, 49, 50
Cho Pyong Ho, 20
Christian Advocate, 13
Christianity
  Catholic, 48, 82
  in Korea, 13, 30, 38, 39, 65-67, 70, 74
  propagation of, 12
  Protestant, 41, 42
  see also Catholics
Confucian culture, 5, 6, 19, 81, 82
  see also Neoconfucianism
Corea, The Hermit Nation, 54-56

Diplomats, 2, 6, 12, 30
Dodge, Ella (Mrs. Henry Appenzeller), 26, 27, 40
Drew Theological Seminary, 11, 26-28, 71, 85, 86
Dutch Reformed Church, 23-25, 27
  Theological Seminary, 23, 85

Other Orbis books . . .

THE MEANING OF MISSION

José Comblin

"This very readable book has made me think, and I feel it will be useful for anyone dealing with their Christian role of mission and evangelism." *New Review of Books and Religion*
ISBN 0-88344-304-X CIP   *Cloth $6.95*

THE GOSPEL OF PEACE AND JUSTICE

Catholic Social Teaching Since Pope John

Presented by Joseph Gremillion

"Especially valuable as a resource. The book brings together 22 documents containing the developing social teaching of the church from *Mater et Magistra* to Pope Paul's 1975 *Peace Day Message on Reconciliation*. I watched the intellectual excitement of students who used Gremillion's book in a justice and peace course I taught last summer, as they discovered a body of teaching on the issues they had defined as relevant. To read Gremillion's overview and prospectus, a meaty introductory essay of some 140 pages, is to be guided through the sea of social teaching by a remarkably adept navigator."

National Catholic Reporter

"An authoritative guide and study aid for concerned Catholics and others." *Library Journal*
ISBN 0-88344-165-9   *Cloth $15.95*
ISBN 0-88344-166-7   *Paper $8.95*

THEOLOGY IN THE AMERICAS

Papers of the 1975 Detroit Conference

Edited by Sergio Torres and John Eagleson

"A pathbreaking book from and about a pathbreaking theological conference, *Theology in the Americas* makes a major contribution to ecumenical theology, Christian social ethics and liberation movements in dialogue." *Fellowship*
ISBN 0-88344-479-8 CIP   *Cloth $12.95*
ISBN 0-88344-476-3   *Paper $5.95*

LOVE AND STRUGGLE
IN MAO'S THOUGHT

Raymond L. Whitehead

"Mao's thoughts have forced Whitehead to reassess his own philosophy and to find himself more fully as a Christian. His well documented and meticulously expounded philosophy of Mao's love and struggle-thought might do as much for many a searching reader." *Prairie Messenger*

ISBN 0-88344-289-2 CIP   *Cloth $8.95*
ISBN 0-88344-290-6   *Paper $3.95*

WATERBUFFALO THEOLOGY

Kosuke Koyama

"This book with its vivid metaphors, fresh imagination and creative symbolism is a 'must' for anyone desiring to gain a glimpse into the Asian mind." *Evangelical Missions Quarterly*

ISBN 0-88344-702-9   *Paper $4.95*

ASIAN VOICES
IN CHRISTIAN THEOLOGY

Edited by Gerald H. Anderson

"A basic sourcebook for anyone interested in the state of Protestant theology in Asia today. I am aware of no other book in English that treats this matter more completely." *National Catholic Reporter*

ISBN 0-88344-017-2   *Cloth $15.00*
ISBN 0-88344-016-4   *Paper $7.95*

FAREWELL TO INNOCENCE

Allan Boesak

"This is an extremely helpful book. The treatment of the themes of power, liberation, and reconciliation is precise, original, and Biblically-rooted. Dr. Boesak has done much to advance the discussion, and no one who is interested in these matters can afford to ignore his important contribution." *Richard J. Mouw, Calvin College*

ISBN 0-88344-130-6 CIP   *Cloth $4.95*

MARX AND THE BIBLE

José Miranda

"An inescapable book which raises more questions than it answers, which will satisfy few of us, but will not let us rest easily again. It is an attempt to utilize the best tradition of Scripture scholarship to understand the text when it is set in a context of human need and misery."

Walter Brueggemann, in Interpretation

ISBN 0-88344-306-6   *Cloth $8.95*
ISBN 0-88344-307-4   *Paper $4.95*

BEING AND THE MESSIAH

The Message of Saint John

José Miranda

"This book could become the catalyst of a new debate on the Fourth Gospel. Johannine scholarship will hotly debate the 'terrifyingly revolutionary thesis that this world of contempt and oppression can be changed into a world of complete selflessness and unrestricted mutual assistance.' Cast in the framework of an analysis of contemporary philosophy, the volume will prove a classic of Latin American theology." *Frederick Herzog, Duke University Divinity School*

ISBN 0-88344-027-X CIP   *Cloth $8.95*
ISBN 0-88344-028-8   *Paper $4.95*

THE GOSPEL IN SOLENTINAME

Ernesto Cardenal

"Upon reading this book, I want to do so many things—burn all my other books which at best seem like hay, soggy with mildew. I now know who (not what) is the church and how to celebrate church in the eucharist. The dialogues are intense, profound, radical. *The Gospel in Solentiname* calls us home."

Carroll Stuhlmueller, National Catholic Reporter

ISBN 0-88344-168-3   *Vol. 1 Cloth $6.95*
ISBN 0-88344-170-5   *Vol. 1 Paper $4.95*
ISBN 0-88344-167-5   *Vol. 2 Cloth $6.95*

THE PRAYERS
OF AFRICAN RELIGION

John S. Mbiti

"We owe a debt of gratitude to Mbiti for this excellent anthology which so well illuminates African traditional religious life and illustrates so beautifully man as the one who prays." *Sisters Today*
ISBN 0-88344-394-5 CIP   *Cloth $7.95*

POLYGAMY RECONSIDERED

Eugene Hillman

"This is by all odds the most careful consideration of polygamy and the attitude of Christian Churches toward it which it has been my privilege to see." *Missiology*
ISBN 0-88344-391-0   *Cloth $15.00*
ISBN 0-88344-392-9   *Paper $7.95*

AFRICAN TRADITIONAL RELIGION

E. Bolaji Idowu

"A great work in the field and closely comparable to Mbiti's *African Religions and Philosophy*. It is worthwhile reading." *The Jurist*
ISBN 0-88344-005-9   *Cloth $6.95*

AFRICAN CULTURE
AND THE CHRISTIAN CHURCH

Aylward Shorter

"An introduction to social and pastoral anthropology, written in Africa for the African Christian Churches." *Western Catholic Reporter*
ISBN 0-88344-004-0   *Paper $6.50*

TANZANIA AND NYERERE

William R. Duggan & John R. Civille

"Sympathetic survey of Tanzania's attempt to develop economically on an independent path." *Journal of World Affairs*
ISBN 0-88344-475-5 CIP   *Cloth $10.95*